20.00

SCHOOL PRAYER AND
OTHER RELIGIOUS ISSUES
IN AMERICAN PUBLIC EDUCATION

GARLAND REFERENCE LIBRARY
OF SOCIAL SCIENCE
(VOL. 291)

SCHOOL PRAYER AND OTHER RELIGIOUS ISSUES IN AMERICAN PUBLIC EDUCATION
A Bibliography

Albert J. Menendez

GARLAND PUBLISHING, INC. • NEW YORK & LONDON
1985

Ref
016.377
M542

Library of Congress Cataloging in Publication Data

Menendez, Albert J.
School prayer and other religious issues in American
public education.

(Garland reference library of social science ; vol.
291)
Includes indexes.
1. Prayer in the public schools—United States—
Bibliography.   2. Religion in the public schools—United
States—Bibliography.   3. Religious education—United
States—Bibliography.   4. Prayer in the public schools—
Law and legislation—United States—Bibliography.
I. Title.   II. Series: Garland reference library of
social science ; v. 291.
Z5815.U5M46   1985   016.377′1   84-48756
[LC405]
ISBN 0-8240-8775-5 (alk. paper)

Cover design by Donna Montalbano

Printed on acid-free, 250-year-life paper
Manufactured in the United States of America

For Shirley

CONTENTS

vii

INTRODUCTION

There are few issues in American life as complex or controversial as the role that religion should play in public schools at the elementary and secondary level. This bibliographical guide attempts to organize the vast amount of material available on this subject.

The material includes nearly 1,600 books, periodical articles, law journal reviews, dissertations, theses, and a few newspaper articles. I have not included pamphlets because they are difficult to locate in most libraries and collections. I have, however, cited additional bibliographies which do include pamphlets.

The opening chapter looks at introductions to and overviews of the subject by a variety of authors. Most of these authors tried to define the context of the subject and discuss its reference points and parameters. Also included are a number of case studies focusing on certain states and the historical development of religion-in-the-school.

The second chapter focuses on attempts at various times and locales to offer instruction in "moral education," "character building," "education for democracy" or similar euphemisms for a kind of watered-down or consensus religiosity.

Chapters three through seven focus exclusively on the issue of formal, prescribed, daily, or devotional prayers in schools. The third chapter looks at some of the history, while the fourth deals with the legal implications, particularly with the epochal decisions of the U.S. Supreme Court in 1962 and 1963. The political dimensions of this issue—and they are many with Ronald Reagan in the White House—are reviewed in the fifth chapter, while polemical writings comprise the sixth and seventh.

What about Bible reading? This issue has engendered untold bitterness since the Philadelphia Riots of 1844 and a Maine Supreme Court decision in 1854 which upheld expulsion of students whose conscience forbade them to read the Protestant version of the Scriptures. The battles over the Good Book as a devotional tool are covered in chapter eight.

But teaching about religion, including the literary aspects of the

Bible, is another question altogether. Exploring how it can be done constitutionally and practically is considered in chapters nine and ten. Releasing pupils for a portion of the day for religion instruction is a constitutionally permissible practice. Holding religious instruction on public school grounds is impermissible. The ramifications of this once-popular but now largely ignored compromise are explored in chapters eleven and twelve.

The "December dilemma" which pluralistic schools now face every Christmas season receives some attention in chapter thirteen. Devotional services and religious Baccalaureate services are explored in the next chapter.

In chapter fifteen we take a look at a new issue, the fast-breaking controversy over the access, equal or otherwise, that religious groups are demanding in public education. The passage of an equal access bill in the U.S. Congress in 1984 does not mean that this issue is dead. It may become the most hotly contested religious issue in American education during the next few years as schools try to implement the legislation.

How does a teacher's personal religion affect teaching and relationships with students? Chapter sixteen explores that question. Chapter seventeen is concerned with the way in which textbooks deal with religious values. The eighteenth chapter shows how Catholics, Protestants, and Jews have related historically to trends in public education. The nineteenth chapter looks at an odd situation: an amalgamation of Catholic parochial and public schools in certain isolated rural communities. The twentieth chapter focuses on "religious garb," the question of whether members of religious orders or communities may wear their distinctive clothing in public schools. That issue, which led to conflict in many state courts from 1896 to 1956, has now returned to Oregon where a state court decision is expected in 1985.

The final chapter includes some additional bibliographies.

As this book was going to press in October 1984, two excellent new books were published. *Religion, the State and Education*, edited by James F. Wood, Jr. (Waco: Baylor University Press) includes nine well-argued essays and a fine bibliography. *Religion in the Public Schools: An Introduction* by Richard C. McMillan (Macon: Mercer University Press) is an important contribution to the continuing dialogue. It includes a comprehensive bibliography. McMillan argues forcefully that "governmentally sponsored and required acts of religious devotion" have no place "in a pluralistic society dedicated to religious freedom."

School Prayer and
Other Religious Issues
in American Public Education

CHAPTER 1
RELIGION IN THE SCHOOLS: GENERAL OVERVIEW

Can religious training be provided in a pluralistic public setting? If so, how? Is there any way to guarantee that the school will not become a promoter of sectarian values? Should religion be there in the first place, or is it an appropriate place when there are 350,000 churches in the land?

These, and numerous subthemes, are dealt with by a varied group of educators and churchmen. Good overviews and introductions are provided by Butts (51), Henry (151), Kliebard (210), Loder (231) and others.

A major portion of this chapter is given over to case studies of various states. Consult the subject index for each state to locate entries in this chapter.

1 American Association of School Administrators. Religion in the Public Schools. New York: Harper and Row, 1964.

2 American Council on Education. The Function of the Public Schools in Dealing with Religion. Washington, D.C.: 1953.

3 ———. The Relation of Religion to Public Education. Washington, D.C.: 1947.

4 ———. Religion and Public Education. Washington, D.C.: 1944.

5 American Jewish Committee. "Religion in Public Education." Religious Education 50 (July 1955): 232-37.

6 American law Reports Annotated. "Sectarianism in Schools." 5ALR (1920): 866-908; 141ALR (1942): 1144-57.

7 Anderson, Richard Vernal. "Religion and the Public Schools of Colorado, An Historical Analysis, 1851-1963." Ed.D. dissertation. University of Colorado, 1965.

8   Anderson, Robert T. "Religion in the Michigan Public
    Schools." School and Society 87 (May 9, 1959): 227-29.

9   Andrews, Charles J. "The Responsibilities and Practices
    of Public Schools in Texas in Dealing with Religion."
    Ed.D. dissertation. North Texas State University,
    1975.

10 Armstead, Edward, Jr. "A Survey of Certain Issues in
    the Relationship Between Religion and Public Education
    in the United States." M.A. thesis. American Univer-
    sity, 1956.

11 Arthur, Charles Ralph. "Religious Education in Public
    Education in the State of Virginia Since 1900." B.D.
    thesis. Duke University, 1941.

12 Axtelle, George E. "Religion, Education, and Culture."
    The Educational Forum 21 (November 1956): 5-17.

13 Baker, John Henry. "Church and State in New Jersey
    Public Education." Ph.D. dissertation. Princeton
    University, 1961.

14 Ballou, Richard Boyd. "Religious Values in Public Educa-
    tion." Religious Education 49 (September-October
    1954): 317-24.

15 Barr, David L. "Religion in the Curriculum." Education
    Leadership 29 (November 1971): 170-73.

16 ———. "What is the School Doing with Religion?"
    Spectrum 47 (November 1971): 8-9.

17 ———, and William E. Collie. "Religion in the Schools:
    The Continuing Controversy." Church and State 34
    (March 1981): 8-16.

18 Beck, Robert H. "Religion in the Public Schools."
    Educational Administration and Supervision 34 (March
    27, 1948): 155-56.

19 Beery, Cleo C. "Public Schools and Religion: The
    Opinions of Nine Eminent Educators." Ed.D. disserta-
    tion. University of Southern California, 1961.

20 Beggs, David W., ed. America's Schools and Churches:
    Partners in Conflict. Bloomington: Indiana Univer-
    sity, 1966.

21 Bell, Sadie. "The Church, the State and Education in
    Virginia." Ph.D. dissertation. University of
    Pennsylvania, 1930.

22 Belnap, Ralph A. "A Study of Religious Education in the
    Wyoming High Schools." M.A. thesis. University of
    Wyoming, 1948.

23 Beman, Lamar Taney. Religious Teaching in the Public
    Schools. New York: H. W. Wilson, 1927.

24 Bennett, W. F. "Religion and the Public Schools."
    Religious Education 65 (July 1970): 341-43.

25 Benson, A. C. "Religious Education in the Public
    Schools." Living Age 250 (August 11, 1906): 366-73.

26 ———. "Religious Teaching in Secondary Schools."
    Contemporary Review 100 (September 1911): 331-43.

27 Binder, R. M. "The Public School and Religion." Journal
    of Educational Sociology 23 (January 1950): 271-77.

28 Blake, Eugene C. "Strategies for Making Adequate Pro-
    vision of Religious Education for All Our Young."
    Religious Education 49 (March 1954): 100-03.

29 Blanshard, Paul. Religion and the Schools. Boston:
    Beacon, 1963.

30 Blashfield, Herbert W. "Religion and the Public School."
    Religious Education 21 (June 1926): 290-95.

31 Bode, Boyd Henry. "Religion and the Public Schools."
    School and Society 67 (March 27, 1948): 225-29.

32 Boger, David A. "The Johnsburg Case: A Study of Reli-
    gion in the Public School." M.S. thesis. Northern
    Illinois University, 1961.

33 Boles, Donald E. The Bible, Religion and the Public
    Schools. Ames: Iowa State University, 1965.

34 ———. The Two Swords. Ames: Iowa State University,
    1965.

35 Bouton, Eugene. "Different Approaches in Dealing with
    Religion in the Public School." Religious Education
    51 (July 1956): 243-45.

36 Bower, William C. "A Critique of the Function of the Public Schools in Dealing with Religion." Religious Education 48 (May 1953): 169-70.

37 ————. "A Proposed Program for Achieving the Role of Religion in Education." Religious Education 50 (July 1955): 211-18.

38 Bradshaw, Emerson O. "Can Religion be Taught in our Public Schools?" Religious Education 35 (January-March 1940): 32-39.

39 Braiterman, Marvin. Religion and the Public Schools. New York: American Jewish Committee, 1958.

40 Brickman, Benjamin. "Reflections on the Issue of Religion and American Public Education." Educational Outlook 30 (March 1956): 79-84.

41 Brickman, William W. "School and the Church-State Question: Examination of Writings on the Problem." School and Society 71 (May 6, 1950): 273-82.

42 ————, and Stanley Lehrer. Religion, Government, and Education. New York: Society for the Advancement of Education, 1961.

43 Brislawn, Maurice John. "Religion and Public Education in the State of Washington." M.A. thesis. Washington State University (Pullman), 1946.

44 Brown, Betty. "Constitutional Law--Religious Liberty in the Schools." Oregon Law Review 18 (December 1938): 122-28.

45 Brown, Elmer E. "Some Relations of Religious Education and Secular Education." Religious Education 2 (October 1907): 121-34.

46 Brown, Francis J. "Studies of Religion in Public Education." Phi Delta Kappan 36 (April 1955): 252-56.

47 Bucher, Charles A. "Religion and Education." New York State Education 41 (December 1953): 215-17.

48 Burrows, Albert H. "Public Schools and the Teaching of Religion." School and Society 88 (April 9, 1960): 179, 182-83.

49 Butler, Harris D., Jr. "Religious Education in the Public Schools of Texas." M.A. thesis. University of Texas, 1952.

50 Butts, R. Freeman. "Church and State in American Education." Teachers College Record 52 (December 1950): 145-57.

51 ———. The American Tradition in Religion and Education. Boston: Beacon, 1950.

52 Buzzard, Lynn R. Schools: They Haven't Got a Prayer. Elgin, Illinois: David C. Cook Publishing Company, 1982.

53 Byrnes, Lawrence. Religion and Public Education. New York: Harper and Row, 1975.

54 "Can our Public Schools do more about Religion? Symposium." Education 125 (November 1942): 245-47, (December 1942): 273-75.

55 Carmichael, A. Max. "What Shall Be Done about Religion in the Public Schools." Progressive Education 30 (April 1953): 161-65.

56 Chandler, C. C. "Religion in the School: What are the Alternatives?" Educational Leadership 23 (February 1966): 369-72.

57 Charters, W. W. "What the Public Schools Can and Cannot Do in Religious Education." International Journal of Religious Education 5 (November 1928): 17+.

58 Chipkin, Israel S. "Approach to the Problem of Religious Education and the Public School." Jewish Education 15 (May 1944): 130-37.

59 ———. "Public School Time for Religious Education." Jewish Education 12 (January 1941): 130-32.

60 "Church and State--The Place of Religion in the Schools of the State of Iowa." Iowa Law Review 49 (Spring 1964): 771-88.

61 Ciarlo, Enrico L. "Religion in the Public Schools." M.S. thesis. Southern Connecticut State College, 1962.

62 Clark, Samuel I. "Religion in Public Education."
    American Association of University Professors, Bulletin
    40 (Winter 1954-1955): 646-56.

63 Clarke, James Ratcliffe. "Church and State Relationships
    in Education in Utah." Ph.D. dissertation. Utah State
    University, 1958.

64 Cocking, W. D. "Public Schools and the Teaching of
    Religion." School Executive 67 (April 1948): 5.

65 Cohen, Jack Joseph. "The Dilemma of Religion in Public
    Education." Ph.D. dissertation. Columbia University,
    1959.

66 Cole, Stewart G., and Leo Trepp. "Religion and the Pub-
    lic Schools--A Symposium." Religious Education 48
    (May-June 1953): 158-68.

67 Coleman, H. Gertrude. "An Inquiry into the Function of
    Religion in the Public Schools of America." M.A.
    thesis. Rhode Island College of Education, 1954.

68 Collier, Robert Lee. "The Kentucky Court of Appeals,
    Religion and the Public Schools, 1891-1960." Ph.D.
    dissertation. University of Kentucky, 1960.

69 Conway, Don. "Religion and Public Education in the
    States." International Journal of Religious Education
    32 (March 1956): 34-40.

70 Cooper, C. C. "What is Religious Education?" School
    and Society 23 (April 3, 1926): 435-38.

71 Costanzo, Joseph F. "Thomas Jefferson, Religious Educa-
    tion and Public Law." Journal of Public Law 8 (Spring
    1959): 81-108.

72 ———. "Religion in Public School Education." Thought
    31 (Summer 1956): 216-44.

73 ———. This Nation Under God: Church, State and
    Schools in America. New York: Herder and Herder, 1964.

74 Cosway, Richard, and Robert A. Toepfer. "Religion and
    the Schools." University of Cincinnati Law Review 17
    (March 1948): 117-43.

75 Cousins, Norman. "Religion and the Schools." Saturday Review 34 (December 29, 1951): 16.

76 Craun, William Author. "Religious Education in the Public Schools." M.A. thesis. University of South Carolina, 1914.

77 Culbertson, J. A. "Religion and the Schools: Some Issues and Action Guides." Theory Into Pracitce 4 (February 1965): 33-39.

78 Culver, Raymond B. Horace Mann and Religion in the Massachusetts Public Schools. New Haven: Yale University Press, 1929.

79 Curry, L. C. "Education and Religion." Kentucky School Journal 21 (December 1942): 15-16.

80 Dawkins, O. C. "Kentucky Blazes a Trail." The Christian Century 67 (September 6, 1950): 1042-44.

81 Dawson, Eugene E. "The Next Decade of Research and Experimentation Relating to Religion and Public Education." Religious Education 52 (July 1957): 298-306.

82 Dierenfield, Richard Bruce. "An Examination of the Current Relationship Between Religion and American Public Schools." Ph.D. dissertation. University of Colorado, 1958.

83 ————. Religion in American Public Schools. Washington, D.C.: Public Affairs Press, 1962.

84 Dinin, Samuel. "Religion and Education." Jewish Education 25 (Summer 1954): 50-54.

85 "Directive on Teaching Religion in Public Schools." Michigan Education Journal 25 (April 1948): 422-23.

86 Downie, Paul S. "The Relation of Religion to Public School Education." M.A. thesis. University of Michigan, 1957.

87 Drachler, Norman. "The Influence of Sectarianism, Non-Sectarianism, and Secularism upon the Public Schools of Detroit and the University of Michigan, 1837-1900." Ph.D. dissertation. University of Michigan, 1951.

88 Draper, Harry Floyd. "Religious Education in New England before 1800." M.A. thesis. Northwestern University, 1921.

89 Duffy, Janet. "Religion in the Public Schools." M.A. thesis. Adelphi College, 1958.

90 Dykstra, D. Ivan. "Religion and Education." Reformed Review 21 (1968): 2-19.

91 Early, Jack Jones. "Religious Practices in the Public Schools of Selected Communities in Kentucky." Ed.D. dissertation. University of Kentucky, 1956.

92 Elliott, Harrison S. "Major Issues in the Proposals to Make Agencies of Public Education Responsible for Teaching Religion." Religious Education 43 (July 1948): 198-200.

93 ———. "The Place of Religion in Elementary and Secondary Education." Religious Education 35 (October 1940): 195-204.

94 ———. "Relationship of Religious Education to Public Education." Jewish Education 13 (September 1941): 92-98.

95 ———. "Religion in the Educational Experience of Children and Youth: A Syllabus." Religious Education 36 (October 1941): 195-211.

96 Engel, David E., ed. Religion in Public Education. Paramus, New Jersey: Paulist, 1974.

97 Ensign, Forest C. "Religious Education and the Public School System." Religious Education 10 (December 1915): 549-58.

98 Esch, I. Lynd. "Appreciation of Religious Values in the Public Schools." Christian Education 29 (June 1946): 274-80.

99 ———. "The Appreciation of Religious Values in the Public Schools." Ph.D. dissertation. University of Southern California, 1942.

100 Felt, Elizabeth. "A Study of Religion in Public Elementary Schools." M.Ed. thesis. Cornell University, 1959.

101 Fey, Harold E. "Religion in Public Education." Christian
     Century 66 (February 23, 1949): 231-33.

102 Finkelstein, Louis. "The Function of the Public Schools
     in Dealing with Religion; Evaluations." Religious
     Education 48 (March 1953): 73-75.

103 Fischer, L. "Teaching-Style and Religion in the Class-
     room." The Educational Forum 32 (January 1968): 211-15.

104 Fisher, Joseph A. "No National School Board: The U.S.
     Supreme Court, Religion and Public Education." Ph.D.
     dissertation. University of Nebraska, 1966.

105 Fister, James Blaine. "Limits of Neutrality for the
     Public Schools in the Teaching of Religion." Inter-
     national Journal of Religious Education 44 (October
     1967): 3-4.

106 Fitzpatrick, Edward A. "Religion in Public Education."
     The American School Board Journal 115 (July 1947):
     31-33.

107 ———. "Religion in Public Education." The American
     School Board Journal 126 (June 1953): 33-34.

108 Flashmeier, William A. "Religious Education and the
     Public Schools." Texas Outlook 36 (August 1952):
     14-15.

109 ———. "Religious Education in the Public Schools of
     Texas." Ph.D. dissertation. University of Texas,
     1955.

110 Forcinelli, Joseph. "School Administration and Religious
     Education in the Public Schools of America." M.A.
     thesis. Claremont College, 1955.

111 Fox, George G. "Religious Education, But Not in Public
     Schools." Religious Education 36 (October-December
     1941): 212-19.

112 Fox, Marvin. "Religion and the Public Schools: A Philo-
     sopher's Analysis." Theory Into Practice 4 (February
     1965): 40-44.

113 ———. "Who is Competent to Teach Religion?" Religious
     Education 54 (March 1959): 112-14.

114 Freehof, Solomon B. "Religion and the Public Schools--
     What to Guard Against." Religious Education 43 (July
     1948): 207-09.

115 Friedman, Lee M. "The Parental Right to Control the
     Religious Education of the Child." Harvard Law Review
     29 (March 1916): 485-500

116 Fuller, Edgar E. "Public Schools and Separation of
     Church and State." School Executive 68 (May 1949):
     11-18.

117 Gaustad, Edwin Scott. "Our National Dilemma: Religion
     and the Schools." Andover Newton Quarterly 5
     (September 1964): 5-15.

118 Geisert, Henry A. "Religion in Education." Education
     43 (November 1922): 129-40.

119 Gesler, Albert Urban. "A Survey of Religious Education
     in the Public Schools of the United States." B.D.
     thesis. Lutheran Theological Seminary, 1932.

120 Gilbert, Arthur. "A Workshop on Religion in the Public
     Schools." Religious Education 50 (July 1955): 225-31.

121 Gladden, Washington. "Religion and the Schools."
     Atlantic Monthly 115 (January 1915): 57-68.

122 Gobbell, Luther L. Church and State Relationships in
     Education in North Carolina Since 1776. Durham: Duke
     University, 1938.

123 Gordis, Robert T., et al. Religion and the Schools.
     Santa Barbara: Fund for the Republic, 1959.

124 Grafflin, Douglas G. "Religious Education for Public
     Schools." The Phi Delta Kappan 28 (December 1946):
     175-76.

125 Graves, Donald Wayne. "An Investigation of Attitudes
     and Practices Regarding Bible Reading and Prayer in
     the Public Schools of Oklahoma." Ed.D. dissertation.
     University of Oklahoma, 1970.

126 Grimshaw, Ivan G. "Religious Education in Public
     Schools." Religious Education 23 (May 1928): 458-62.

127 Gross, Elbert. "The Scarsdale Controversy, 1948-1954."
     Ph.D. dissertation. Columbia University, 1958.

128 Halberstadt, L. C. "Should Religion be Taught in Public
     Schools?" The Nation's Schools 43 (September 1944):
     47-48.

129 Hall, Arthur Jackson. Religious Education in the Public
     Schools of the State and City of New York. Chicago:
     University of Chicago, 1914.

130 Hall, Ida Mildred. "A Survey of the Organized Religious
     Education Facilities Offered to the Child of Elementary
     School Age in Wichita, Kansas." M.A. thesis. Univer-
     sity of Wichita, 1930.

131 Hall, William T. "An Enduring Controversy--The Place of
     Religion in Public Education." The Educational Leader
     19 (October 1, 1955): 5-18.

132 Hamant, Nancy Russell. "An Historical Perspective on
     Religious Practices in Selected Ohio City School
     Districts." Ed.D. dissertation. University of
     Cincinnati, 1967.

133 Hardie, C. D. "Religion and Education." Educational
     Theory 8 (Summer 1968): 199-223.

134 Hardon, John A. "Religion in the Public Schools."
     Catholic Educational Review 56 (May 1958): 289-98.

135 Hardy, Marjorie. "Religious Education in a Kindergarten-
     Primary School." Childhood Education 8 (February
     1932): 301-04.

136 Harner, Kevin C. Religion's Place in General Education.
     Richmond: John Knox Press, 1949.

137 Harris, William T. "The Church, the State, and the
     School." The North American Review 132 (September
     1881): 215-27.

138 ———. "Religious Instruction in the Public Schools."
     Independent 55 (August 6, 1903): 1841-43.

139 Hart, J. K. "Religion in Schools." The Survey 53
     (March 15, 1925): 748-49.

140   Hauser, Conrad Augustine. "Hands Off the Public Schools?"
      Religious Education 37 (March-April 1942): 99-104.

141   ———. Teaching Religion in the Public School. New
      York: Round Table Press, 1942.

142   Havighurst, Robert J. "Religious Education and the
      Schools." The School Review 49 (May 1941): 324-26.

143   Hay, Clyde Lemont. The Blind Spot in American Public
      Education. New York: Macmillan, 1950.

144   ———. "Our Bifurcated Educational System." Religious
      Education 43 (March-April 1948): 72-74.

145   Hays, Arthur G. "Bootlegging Religion." The Nation 124
      (February 9, 1927): 129-40.

146   Hayward, P. R. "The Place of God in Education."
      Religious Education 34 (October 1939): 202-08.

147   Hegland, Martin. Christianity in Education. Minneapolis:
      Augsburg, 1954.

148   Heller, Bernard. "Teaching of Non-Sectarian Religion in
      the Public Schools." Jewish Education 15 (May 1944):
      138-47.

149   Helmreich, Ernst C. Religion and the Maine Schools: An
      Historical Approach. Brunswick, Maine: Bureau for
      Research in Municipal Government, 1960.

150   Henry, Carl F. H. "Christian Responsibility in Educa-
      tion." Christianity Today I (May 27, 1957): 11-14.

151   Henry, Virgil. The Place of Religion in Public Schools.
      New York: Harper and Row, 1950.

152   ———. "Religion in the Curriculum." Illinois Educa-
      tion 37 (January 1949): 175-77.

153   Herrick, V. E. "Religion in the Public Schools of
      America." Elementary School Journal 46 (November 1945):
      119-26.

154   Hill, Thomas Paul. "Religion in the Classroom." Ph.D.
      dissertation. Ohio State University, 1966.

155 Hillis, Lewis B. "Trends in the Relation of Education and Religion." Religious Education 27 (June 1932): 541-47.

156 Hites, Laird T. "Recent Legislation on Religion and the Public Schools." Religious Education 20 (August 1925): 292-97.

157 Hochwalt, Frederick G. "The Function of the Public Schools in Dealing with Religion, Evaluation." Religious Education 48 (March 1954): 75-77.

158 Hollingsworth, Glen Howard. "A Study of Religious Education in the Public Schools of the State of Ohio." M.Ed. dissertation. Kent State University, 1949.

159 Holmes, Henry W. "God in the Public Schools." Atlantic Monthly 166 (July 1940): 99-105.

160 Holmes, Jesse H. "The Public School and the Church: How Can Each Help the Other?" Religious Education 5 (April 1910): 37-45.

161 Humble, Earl Raymond. "Religious Instruction and Activities in the Public Schools of Texas--A Contemporary Survey." S.T.D. dissertation. Southwestern Baptist Theological Seminary, 1960.

162 ———. "Religious Instruction and Activities in Texas Public Schools." A Journal of Church and State 2 (November 1960): 117-36.

163 Hunt, Rolfe Lanier. "Christian Concern for the Public Schools." Social Action 24 (February 1958): 4-10.

164 ———. "How Far Can Public Schools Go?" International Journal of Religious Education 30 (April 1954): 20-22.

165 ———. "How Shall Public Schools Deal with Religion?" International Journal of Religious Education 32 (October 1955): 8-10.

166 ———. "Public Education and Religion: A Study Document for Churches on the National Conference on Religion and Education." International Journal of Religious Education 32 (March 1956): 21-52.

167 Hunt, Rolfe Lanier. "Relation of Religion in Public
     Education." Religious Education 55 (July 1960): 265-69.

168 ―――. "Religion and Public Education." School and
     Society 89(May 1961): 230-33.

169 ―――. "Religion in Public Education." Phi Delta
     Kappan 36 (April 1955): 243-44, 256.

170 ―――. "Religion: Its Relation to Public Education."
     Nation's Schools 67 (March 1961): 59-65, 106, 108, 110,
     112.

171 ―――. "These Things Public Schools May Do." Inter-
     national Journal of Religious Education 42 (April
     1966): 16-17.

172 Hurley, Mark J. Church-State Relationships in Education
     in California. Washington, D.C.: Catholic University
     of America, 1948.

173 Huzica, Sister Mary P. "Some of the Founding Fathers
     and Their Ideas of Religion in Education." M.A.
     thesis. St. John College (Cleveland), 1955.

174 "Instruction in Religion in Relation to Public Education--
     A Booklist." Religious Education 10 (December 1915):
     613-24.

175 "Is There a Place for Religious Education in the Public
     Schools?" The Andover Newton Quarterly 5 (September
     1964): 3-48.

176 Jackson, Jerome Case, and Constantine Malmberg. Reli-
     gious Education and the State. Garden City: Doubleday,
     Doran, 1928.

177 Jacobson, Philip. Religion and Public Education: A
     Guide for Discussion. New York: American Jewish
     Committee, 1963.

178 Jarman, Bernice Herman. "Religious Education and the
     Public School." School and Society 67 (January 17,
     1948): 44-46.

179 Johnson, Alvin D. "Religion in Public Education." M.A.
     thesis. University of Connecticut, 1955.

180 Johnson, F. Ernest. "A Guide to Group Study of Religion and Public Education." Religious Education 48 (November 1953): 422-30.

181 ———, ed. American Education and Religion. New York: Harper and Row, 1952.

182 ———. "Church, State and School." Education 71 (February 1951): 353-57.

183 ———. "The Controversial Question of Religion and Public Education." School and Society 61 (June 16, 1945): 398-99.

184 ———. "Has Religious Teaching a Place in Public Education?" International Journal of Religious Education 16 (October 1939): 8-9.

185 ———. "Interpreting Religion in Education." Religious Education 45 (July 1950): 203-06.

186 ———. "Issues Emerging in Religious and General Education." Religious Education 37 (November 1942): 356-58.

187 ———. "The Place of Religion in Public Education." Education 64 (May 1944): 521-23.

188 ———. "Public Education and Religion." Christianity and Crisis 17 (July 20, 1958): 187-89.

189 ———. "Religion and Education." Teachers College Record 57 (March 1956): 378-85.

190 ———. "Religion and Public Education." Christianity and Crisis 20 (September 19, 1960): 127-28.

191 ———. "Religion and Public Education." National Association of Secondary-School Principals, Bulletin 31 (April 1947): 95-102.

192 ———. "Religion and Public Education." Social Action 24 (February 1958): 11-14.

193 ———. "Religion and the Schools—What Can We Hope For?" Religious Education 43 (July 1948): 201-05.

194 ———. "Religion in Education in the Postwar World." Teachers College Record 44 (December 1942): 160-68.

195   Johnson, G. "Religion in Education." The Catholic
      Educational Review 30 (January 1932): 8-14

196   Jordan, Charles F. "Views of the National Education
      Association on the Relation of the Public Schools to
      Religious Education." M.A. thesis. Loyola College,
      1954.

197   Judson, H. P. "Religion in the Public Schools."
      Elementary School Teacher 9 (January 1909): 223-32.

198   Kallas, James. "Christ in the Classroom." Christianity
      Today 12 (1968): 1119-21.

199   Kallen, Horace Meyer. "Churchmen's Claims on the Public
      School." Nation's Schools 29 (May 1942): 49-50.

200   Karpas, Melvin Ronald. "The Schools and Religion: A
      Study to Identify the Advocates of Religious Instruc-
      tion in the Public Schools." Journal of Human Relations
      13 (First Quarter 1965): 13-20.

201   Kelley, Robert L. "The School and Church Co-operating."
      Religious Education 10 (December 1915): 540-48.

202   Kenny, J. J. "Religious Education in the High School."
      National Catholic Educational Association, Proceedings
      (1932): 471-79.

203   Keohane, R. E. "Religion and Education." The School
      Review 55 (November 1947): 511-13.

204   Kepner, Charles W. "The School Challenges the Church."
      School and Society 52 (September 21, 1940): 215-19.

205   Kilpatrick, William H. "Religion in Education: The
      Issues." Progressive Education 26 (February 1949):

206   ———. "Some Issues in Religion and Education."
      Progressive Education 33 (September 1956): 139-40.

207   Kindred, L. W. "Religious Influences in Public Schools."
      Nation's Schools 22 (December 1938): 35-36.

208 Kizer, G. A. "Religion = Education: Cooperation or
     Conflict?" School and Society 99 (March 1971): 152-56.

209 Klain, Z. "The Teaching of Religion." School and
     Society 51 (June 29, 1940): 781-82.

210 Kliebard, Herbert M., ed. Religion and Education in
     America: A Documentary History. Scranton,
     Pennsylvania: International Textbook Company, 1969.

211 Knoff, Gerald E. "The Aims of Religious Education."
     The Phi Delta Kappan 31 (October 1949): 71-75.

212 Knox, W. J. "The Public School as a Factor in Religious
     Education." Religious Education 9 (February 1915):
     60-64.

213 Kramer, John George. "A Critical Analysis of the Major
     Arguments Against the Teaching of Religion in the
     Public Schools." Ph.D. dissertation. Ohio State
     University, 1953.

214 Kucera, Daniel William. Church-State Relationships in
     Education in Illinois. Washington, D.C.: Catholic
     University of America Press, 1955.

215 Ladd, Edward T. "Public Education and Religion."
     Journal of Public Law 13 (1964): 310-42.

216 Landry, Sabin., Jr. "A Consideration of the Place of
     Religion in Public Education." Review and Expositor
     15 (April 1959): 144-65.

217 LaRue, D. W. "Church and the Public School." Educa-
     tional Review 37 (May 1909): 468-76.

218 Lawler, Harold Joseph. "Should Religion be Taught in
     Public Schools?" M.S. thesis. Southern Connecticut
     State College, 1960.

219 Lekachman, Robert. "Can the Public School Be Neutral?
     An Unreligious View." Education Digest 24 (October
     1959): 18-21.

220 Lennon, Brother C. Andrew (Martin). "A Study of the
     Struggle to Maintain Religion in Education in Massa-
     chusetts During the Years, 1820-1850." M.A. thesis.
     Fordham University, 1937.

221 LePelley, S. "Religion in Secondary Schools." Contem-
     porary Review 100 (October 1911): 532-37.

222 Leuba, James H. "The Teaching of Religion in the
     Schools." Teachers College Journal 15 (January 1944):
     54+.

223 Lewis, Edwin C., et al. "Do Present Plans Endanger Our
     Religious Liberties?" Religious Education 11 (June
     1916): 259-76.

224 Lewiston, James. "Religious Education in Some Selected
     High Schools of Iowa." M.A. thesis. Drake University,
     1956.

225 Lieberman, Abraham I. "A History of Religious Influence
     in the Public Schools of New York." M.Ed. thesis.
     City College of New York, 1930.

226 Liggett, Robert L. "An Investigation of Certain Aspects
     of Religious Education in the Public Schools of
     Indiana." Ph.D. dissertation. Indiana University,
     1950.

227 Linton, Clarence. "The Function of the Public Schools
     in Dealing with Religion." Religious Education 48
     (March 1953): 67-72.

228 Little, Lawrence Calvin. "The Relation of Religion to
     Contemporary Public Education." Religious Education
     46 (July 1951): 237-50.

229 ————. "Religion in the Public Schools." Adult
     Student 18 (September 1959): 10-13.

230 ————. "Syllabus on Religion and Public Education."
     Religious Education 44 (May 1949): 163-76.

231 Loder, James E. Religion and the Public Schools. New
     York: Association Press, 1965.

232 Looft, Robert Dean. "Religious Instruction Practices
     in Public Schools of Seven Mid-west States." Ph.D.
     dissertation. Iowa State University of Science and
     Technology, 1966.

233 Lookstein, Joseph H. "Religion and the Public Schools."
     Jewish Education 21 (Winter 1949): 38-43.

234 Lopez, R. Alfonso. "The Principle of Separation of Church and State as Observed by the Public Schools of Puerto Rico from 1898 to 1952." Ph.D. dissertation. New York University, 1971.

235 Madden, Ward. Religious Values in Education. New York: Harper and Row, 1951.

236 Madigan, Lawrence M. "Religion in the Public Schools." Catholic World 189 (June 1959): 201-07.

237 Mahoney, Charles J. The Relation of the State to Religious Education in Early New York, 1633-1825. Washington, D.C.: Catholic University of America, 1941.

238 Mandel, Bernard. "Religion and the Public Schools of Ohio." Ohio State Archaeological and Historical Quarterly 58 (1949): 185-206.

239 Manning, Norman Pryor. "Religious Training in the Public Schools of Cobb County, Georgia." B.D. dissertation. Emory University, 1931.

240 Martin, A. E. "Keep God in Our Public Schools." Texas Outlook 43 (April 1959): 24-25.

241 Martin, Frank T. "The Michigan School Controversy." M.A. thesis. The Catholic University of America, 1949.

242 Martin, Renwick Harper. "Fourth R in American Education." Christianity Today 1 (September 2, 1957): 11-12.

243 Mason, Sister Mary Paul. Church-State Relationships in Education in Connecticut, 1633-1953. Washington, D.C.: Catholic University of America Press, 1953.

244 Mattox, Fount William. "The Teaching of Religion in the Public Schools." Ph.D. dissertation. George Peabody College, 1948.

245 Maxwell, Samuel A. "Religious Education and the Public School: A Study in the Problems of Correlation." M.A. thesis. University of Kentucky, 1927.

246 Mayer, Frederick. "Education and Religion." Phi Delta Kappan 36 (April 1955): 245-48.

247 McAuliffe, Mary F. "A Study of the Present Status of Religious Education in Public Schools and a Plan for Its Extension." Ph.D. dissertation. Boston College, 1935.

248 McClanahan, Burl Austin. "School Board Policy, and Its Implementation Relating to Religious Activities in Missouri Public Schools." Ed.D. dissertation. University of Missouri, 1965.

249 McCorkle, H. L. "Religion in the Public Schools: An Interview with Philip H. Phenix." Spectrum 45 (March 1969): 4-7.

250 McCormick, Leo Joseph. Church-State Relationships in Education in Maryland. Washington, D.C.: Catholic University of America, 1942.

251 McDowell, John B., and Theodore Powell. Religion and Education. New York: National Conference of Christians and Jews, 1962.

252 McKibben, Frank M. "Religious Teaching in Public Education." International Journal of Religious Education 16 (November 1939): 12+.

253 McQuaid, B. J. "Religion in Schools." The North American Review 132 (April 1881): 332-44.

254 Mellenbruck, Pearl Leslie. "The Place and Legitimate Function of Religion in Education." M.A. thesis. University of Kansas, 1920.

255 Meyer, Carl S. "Religion in the Public Schools." Concordia Theological Monthly 28 (February 1957): 81-109.

256 Meyer, Harry Louis. "Religious Education in the Public Schools of the State of Michigan (1669 to 1869)." M.A. thesis. University of Chicago, 1919.

257 Meyer, John B. Religion in the School Curriculum. Boston: R. D. Badger, 1927.

258 Michaelsen, Robert. Piety in the Public School. New York: The Macmillan Company, 1970.

259 Michaelsen, Robert. "The Public Schools and 'America's
    Two Religions.'" Journal of Church and State 8
    (Autumn 1966): 380-400.

260 Miller, James Blair. "Patterns of Disagreement Concern-
    ing Religion in Relation to Public Education in the
    United States." Ph.D. dissertation. Indiana Univer-
    sity, 1955.

261 Miller, William Lee. "The Fight Over America's Fourth
    'R'." The Reporter 14 (March 22, 1956): 20-26.

262 Moehlman, Conrad H. School and Church, the American
    Way. New York: Harper and Row, 1944.

263 Mol, J. J. "Religion and Education in Sociological
    Perspective." Religious Education 60 (May 1965):
    238-43.

264 Mueller, Donald Dean. "Religious Education in the Public
    Schools from an Evangelical Point of View." M.R.E.
    thesis. Asbury Theological Seminary, 1960.

265 Mulford, Herbert B. "As Public Education Defaults on
    Religion." School and Society 64 (December 21, 1946):
    443-44.

266 ———. "A New Spiritual Chapter in Public Education."
    American School Board Journal 131 (July 1955): 29-30.

267 ———. "A Pattern for Religion in Public Education."
    Religious Education 49 (September-October 1954): 333-36.

268 ———. "Public School Boards Face Dilemma in Religious
    Education." Religious Education 43 (March-April 1948):
    68-71.

269 ———. "This is a Religious Nation." American School
    Board Journal 124 (February 1952): 39-40.

270 ———. "Toward a New Spiritual Formula for Public
    Education." American School Board Journal 128 (May
    1954): 33-34.

271 Mullin, John Bernard. "Religious Education and the
    American Public School." M.A. thesis. Boston College,
    1929.

272 Munn, Merton Deming, and Dayton T. Yoder. "Teaching
     Religion in Public Schools? Yes." M. D. Munn.
     "Teaching Religion in Public Schools? No." D. T.
     Yoder. Religious Education 37 (July-August 1942):
     213-20.

273 Murphy, E. J. "Church-State Controversy and Your
     Schools." School Management 10 (October 1967): 117-120+.

274 Murra, Wilbur Fim. "An Inquiry into the Role of Religion
     in the Public Schools of a Secular State." Ph.D.
     dissertation. University of Minnesota, 1958.

275 Nachlas, Morton DeCorcey. "A Study of Attitudes of
     Parents, School Administrators and Clergymen Toward
     Religious Instruction in the High School." Ph.D.
     dissertation. Ohio State University, 1949.

276 ———. "Study of Attitudes of School Administrators
     Toward Religious Instruction in the High School."
     National Association of Secondary School Principals
     Bulletin 36 (October 1952): 95-100.

277 Nathanson, Jerome. "The Battle for Free Schools--The
     Foot in the Door." The Nation 173 (November 17, 1951):
     423-25.

278 ———. "Religion in Public Education." Progressive
     Education 33 (September 1956): 151+.

279 "A National Institute of Religious Education." School
     and Society 21 (January 31, 1925): 135-36.

280 National School Public Relations Association. Religion
     and the Schools. Washington, D.C.: 1970.

281 Nelson, Thomas L. "The Fourth 'R'--Religion--in Educa-
     tion." Religious Education 51 (January 1956): 40-42.

282 Niebuhr, Reinhold. "Religion and Education." Religious
     Education 48 (November 1953): 371-73.

283 Nielsen, Niels C., Jr. "Religion and Public Education."
     America 108 (June 8, 1963): 830-31.

284 Nordberg, G. S. "Present Status of Religious Education
     in Connection with the American Elementary and Second-
     ary Schools." M.A. thesis. University of North
     Dakota, 1924.

285 Norton, Albert Charles. "Christianity and our Schools." Christianity Today 2 (May 12, 1958): 8-10.

286 Norton, John K. "What Should Be the Relation of Religion and Public Education?" Teachers College Record 56 (October 1954): 10-15.

287 O'Connell, J. J. "Religion and the Public Schools." Washington Education 75 (February 1964): 18-21+.

288 O'Donnell, William Charles. Creed and Curriculum: Can the Essentials of Religious Faith and Practice Be Taught in the Public Schools of the United States? New York: Eaton and Mains, 1914.

289 Olds, G. A. "Fourth R." American Association of School Administrators Official Report (1965): 42-50.

290 O'Neill, James M. "Religion and Education: The American Tradition." America 83 (September 1950): 579-81+.

291 ———. "Religious Education and American Democracy." National Catholic Educational Association, Proceedings (1952): 45-49.

292 Oppewal, D. "Religion and Public Education: An Emerging Quandry." The Educational Forum 31 (March 1967): 323-331.

293 "Opportunity for Religious Education of School Children under the Gary Plan." Current Opinion 59 (December 1915): 419-20.

294 Ostdiek, J. H. "Religious Instruction of Public-High-School Pupils." The Catholic School Journal 36 (September 1936): 228-30.

295 Palmer, Raymond Roderick. "Should Religion be Taught in the Public Schools." Social Studies 49 (January 1958): 17-20.

296 Parker, Alfred E. "Consensus on Religion in the Schools." Phi Delta Kappan 38 (January 1957): 145-47.

297 Parkinson, William D. "The School and the Church." The School Review 13 (November 1905): 661-77.

298 Pepper, Ray E. "Religion in Public Education." M.A.
     thesis. Ohio State University, 1957.

299 Pfeffer, Leo. "Religion, Education and the Constitution."
     Lawyers Guild Review 8 (May 1948): 387-99.

300 Phenix, Philip H. "Religion in American Public Educa-
     tion." Teachers College Record 57 (October 1955):
     26-31.

301 ———. "Religion in Public Education: Principles and
     Issues." Journal of Church and State 14 (Autumn
     1972): 415-30.

302 ———. Religious Concerns in Contemporary Education.
     New York: Teachers College, Columbia University, 1959.

303 ———. "The Religious Element in Education." The
     Educational Forum 26 (November 1961): 15-22.

304 Pleasants, S. A. "Church and State in a Public School
     System." The Clearing House 34 (January 1960): 277-78.

305 ———. "Religion in the School: A Historical Account
     of Church and State in the Public Classroom." The
     Clearing House 37 (December 1962): 218-21.

306 Pope, Liston. "Religion and Our Schools." American
     Magazine 153 (May 1952): 24-25, 110-14.

307 Pound, C. W. "Religious Education During School Hours."
     The Elementary School Journal 28 (September 1927): 6-8.

308 Pratt, J. W. "Religious Conflict in the Development of
     the New York City Public School System." History of
     Education Quarterly 5 (1965): 110-20.

309 Presley, Earl Christian. "The Place of Religion in
     Primary and Secondary Education in America." M.A.
     thesis. Emory University, 1941.

310 "Public Education and Religion: A Study Document. . ."
     International Journal of Religious Education 72 (March
     1956): 21-52.

311 "The Public School and Religious Education." Religious
     Education 49 (March 1954): 143-46.

312 "Public Schools Can Teach Religion!" Christian Century
65 (April 28, 1948): 374-76.

313 Punke, Merlo J. "Religion in American Public Schools."
Religious Education 52 (March 1957): 133-40.

314 ————. "Religious Issues in American Public Education."
Law and Contemporary Problems 20 (Winter 1955): 138-68.

315 Ramsey, Paul. "How Shall We Sing the Lord's Song in a
Pluralistic Land?" Journal of Public Law 13 (1964):
353-400.

316 Read, Gerald. "Concerns for Religion and Education."
Phi Delta Kappan 36 (April 1955): 267-68.

317 Reavis, George H. "An Educational Platform for the
Public Schools." International Journal of Religious
Education 34 (May 1958): 14-27.

318 ————. "The Schools and Religion." Religious Education
51 (July 1956): 255-58.

319 Reed, George E. "Another Tradition at Stake." Catholic
Action 32 (February 1950): 4-5.

320 "The Relation of Religion to Public Education." International Journal of Religious Education 36 (April 1960):
21-36.

321 "Religion and Education; A Symposium." Progressive
Education 33 (September 1956): 139-51+.

322 "Religion and Public Education--A Symposium." Religious
Education 44 (November-December 1949): 323-47.

323 "Religion and Public Education: A Symposium." Religious
Education 55 (July 1960): 265-96.

324 "Religion and the Public Schools." The Catholic World
122 (March 1926): 842-44.

325 "Religion and the Public Schools." Vanderbilt Law Review
20 (October 1967): 1078 ff.

326 "Religion and the Public Schools: A Symposium." Religious Education 48 (March 1953): 67-80; 48 (May 1953):
158-70.

327 "Religion and the Public Schools: A Symposium." Religious Education 51 (July 1956): 243-75.

328 "Religion and the Public Schools: Symposium." Religious Education 61 (January 1966): 13-29.

329 "Religion in American Public Schools: Symposium." Religious Education 54 (March 1969): Entire issue.

330 "Religion in Public Education." Biblical World 31 (April 1908): 243-46.

331 "Religion in Public Education." Catholic Action 29 (December 1947): 13-15.

332 "Religion in Public Education [Indianapolis Plan]." The Christian Century 72 (January 1955): 102-04.

333 "Religion in Public Schools Remains Live Issue." The Christian Century 76 (February 11, 1959): 157-58.

334 "Religion in the Public Schools." Christian Century 58 (March 19, 1941): 384-85.

335 "Religion in the Public Schools." The New Republic 5 (November 13, 1915): 33-34.

336 "Religion in the Public Schools." Outlook 86 (June 8, 1907): 275-76.

337 "Religion in the Public Schools--A Symposium." Religious Education 50 (July-August 1955): 211-46.

338 "Religion in the Public Schools: A Symposium." Religious Education 59 (November 1964): 443-79.

339 "Religion in the Public Schools: A Symposium." Religious Education 64 (May 1969): Entire issue.

340 "Religion in the Schools: Does God Belong?" America 94 (December 10, 1955): 296-97.

341 "Religious Education and the Public Schools." Religious Education 43 (March 1948): 65-74.

342 "Religious Education and the Public Schools--A Symposium." Religious Education 43 (July-August 1948): 193-228.

343 "Religious Education in the Public Schools." National
     Education Association, Research Bulletin 35 (December
     1957): 169-71.

344 "Religious Education of Public School Pupils in Wisconsin."
     Wisconsin Law Review 1953 (March 1953): 181-225.

345 Resnik, Reubin. "Religious Education in Buffalo and
     Erie County." Religious Education 56 (September 1961):
     348-50.

346 Reutter, E. E. "Religion and Public Schools." Education
     Digest 39 (December 1973): 26-28.

347 Reynolds, Clarence Eliot. "Basis of Cooperation in
     Religious Education Between Religion and the Public
     Schools." Ed.D. dissertation. Stanford University,
     1945.

348 Rice, Arthur H. "Religion: Its Relation to Public
     Education." Nation's Schools 67 (March 1961): 59-65.

349 Entry deleted.

350 ———. "What Shall Schools Teach about Religion?"
     Nation's Schools 44 (July 1949): 20.

351 Rich, Abel S. "A Survey of the Amount of Religious
     Education Received by the Boys and Girls of Brigham
     City [Utah], Ages Four to Eighteen, During the Year
     1924." M.S. thesis. Brigham Young University, 1926.

352 Richardson, N. E. The Christ of the Classroom. New
     York: Macmillan, 1931.

353 Rogers, Vincent R., and Bruce Burnes. "Religion in the
     Classroom; Another Look." The Phi Delta Kappan 46
     (October 1964): 84-86.

354 Roper, John Caswell. Religious Aspects of Education.
     Nashville: Cokesbury Press, 1926.

355 Rosenfield, H. N. "Separation of Church and State in
     the Public Schools." University of Pittsburgh Law
     Review 22 (March 1961): 561 ff.

356 Russo, Aida Adrienne. "Religion in the History of
     Education in the City of New York, 1623-1842." M.A.
     thesis. Hunter College, 1942.

357 Rutter, C. K. "Religion and School Teaching." Confer-
     ence of Educational Associations, Report (1949):
     280-85.

358 Ryan, Carl J. "Religion and Public Education." Catholic
     Educational Review 57 (November 1959): 532-36.

359 Sackett, Frederick D. "A History of Legislation Affect-
     ing Religious Education in the Elementary and Secondary
     Schools of Texas." M.A. thesis. The Catholic Univer-
     sity of America, 1952.

360 Saveth, Edward N. "Religion and the Public Schools."
     American Jewish Yearbook 53 (1952): 118-25.

361 Schisler, John Q. "Religion and the Public Schools."
     Religion in Life 21 (Winter 1951-1952): 83-93.

362 Scholl, Carolyn S. "Religion and Public Education: An
     Investigation of Existing Policies." M.A. thesis.
     Adelphi College, 1955.

363 Schroeder, H. H. "Religious Element in the Public
     Schools." Educational Review 37 (April 1909):
     375-89.

364 Seckinger, Richard K. "Relation of the State to Reli-
     gious Education in Pennsylvania, 1776-1874." Ed.D.
     dissertation. Teachers College, Columbia University,
     1952.

365 Seitz, W. C. "Religion in Elementary and Secondary
     Education: Some Lay Opinions." Religious Education
     36 (January 1941): 35-42.

366 Seramur, Sister Clarita. "The Place Religion Holds in
     Our Public School System Today." Catholic Educational
     Review 41 (June 1943): 347-53.

367 Seyfert, Frederick, Jr. "Religion in Public Education."
     M.A. thesis. Allegheny College, 1958.

368 Seyfert, W. C. "New Interest in Religious Education."
     The School Review 53 (June 1945): 316-18.

369 "Shall Religious Instruction Be Given in the Public
    Schools?" Biblical World 53 (March 1919): 195-97.

370 Shattuck, George E. "Religious Education in the Schools?"
    Schools and Society 53 (March 22, 1941): 372-73.

371 Sheehy, Howard S., Jr. "A Study of the Moral, Spiritual,
    and Religious Education Policies in Selected Kansas
    Public Schools." M.A. thesis. University of Kansas,
    1960.

372 Sheerin, John B. "Religion in the Public Schools."
    Homiletic and Pastoral Review 56 (June 1956): 723-27.

373 Sheldon, Charles W. "Can Religion be Taught?" The
    Atlantic Monthly 136 (October 1925): 467-72.

374 Shelton, H. S. "Religion in the Schools." Political
    Quarterly 16 (January 1945): 1-12.

375 Sherwood, H. N. "The State and Religious Teaching."
    Scribners' Magazine 78 (August 1925): 202-07.

376 "Should There be Prayer in Public Schools? GH Poll;
    with Statements by E. Dirksen and D. Hunter." Good
    Housekeeping 164 (March 1967): 28+.

377 Sibley, L. A. "How Can Children Get Adequate Religious
    Education?" The Instructor 74 (February 1965): 30+.

378 Siegel, R. Lawrence. "Church-State Separation and the
    Public Schools." Progressive Education 26 (February
    1949): 103-11.

379 Singer, S. A. "Church and School: The Problem Revis-
    ited." Religious Education 65 (July 1970): 352-58.

380 Sisson, Edward O. "The Public School System." Religious
    Education 23 (September 1928): 694-98.

381 ———. "Teaching Religion in Public School is Playing
    with Fire." Nation's Schools 35 (June 1945): 43-44.

382 Sizer, Theodore R., ed. Religion and Public Education.
    Boston: Houghton Mifflin Company, 1967.

383 Smith, Elvin W. "Current Experiments in the Integration
    of Religious Education with the Public School." B.D.
    thesis. Church Divinity School of the Pacific, 1943.

384   Smith, Elwyn A. "How Professor Ramsey Can Sing the
        Lord's Song. . ." *Journal of Public Law* 13 (1964):
        401-16.

385   Smith, H. G. "Religion in Public Schools." *The High
        School Teacher* 7 (March 1931): 95-97+.

386   Smith, J. W. D. "The Place of Religion in Education."
        Contemporary Review 149 (January 1936): 88-95.

387   Smith, Maude E. Wiggs. "State Attitudes Toward Reli-
        gious Education." M.A. thesis. Vanderbilt Univer-
        sity, 1928.

388   Smith, Sherman M. *Religious Education in Massachusetts.*
        Syracuse: 1926.

389   Southcott, Lyall W. "Religion and Education--Past,
        Present and Future." *Teachers College Journal* 15
        (January 1944): 68-69.

390   Southworth, William D. "Religion and the Public Schools."
        Clearing House 32 (May 1958): 515-16.

391   Speer, James Frederick. "Role of Religion in American
        Education." M.R.E. thesis. Biblical Seminary in New
        York, 1931.

392   Spina, Joseph P. "Religion and Public Education in the
        United States." M.Ed. thesis. University of Buffalo,
        1951.

393   Spivey, Robert A. "A New Shape for Religion and Public
        Education in Changing Times." *Journal of Church and
        State* 14 (Autumn 1972): 441-56.

394   Spivey, Robert A. "Religion and Public School Educa-
        tion: A Plan for the Future." *Journal of Church and
        State* 10 (Spring 1968): 193-205.

395   Squires, Vernon P. "Why Ask the State to Give School
        Credits for Religious Instruction?" *Religious Educa-
        tion* 11 (December 1915): 512-17.

396   Stanley, W. O. "Freedom of Conscience, Religion, and
        the Public Schools." *The Educational Forum* 29 (May
        1965): 407-15.

397   Starbuck, Edsin D. "Religion in General Education."
        Educational Review 27 (January 1904): 53-59.

398 "The Status of Religious Education in the Public Schools." NEA Journal 38 (November 1949): 610-11.

399 Stewart, John T. "Religion in the Schools." Christian Century 76 (August 26, 1959): 980.

400 Stoff, Sheldon. "A Program to Teach about Religion in the Public School for Which Consensus of Agreement from Leaders of the Major Religions Has Been Sought." M.Ed. thesis. Cornell University, 1962.

401 ―――. "How Can the Public Schools Manage Religious Issues?" The Clearing House 38 (January 1964): 271-74.

402 Story, M. L. "Religion and the Core Curriculum." Religious Education 47 (January 1952): 19-20.

403 Stump, Lawrence M. "Present Tendencies in the Teaching of Religion in the Public Schools of the United States." Ph.D. dissertation. University of Arizona, 1946.

404 Sullivan, Russell N. "Religious Education in the Schools." Law and Contemporary Problems 14 (Winter 1949): 92-112.

405 Swailes, Elizabeth Baxter. "Religious Education in the Life of the New York Public School Child of Today." M.S. thesis. Hunter College, 1936.

406 Swomley, John M. Religion, the State and the Schools. New York: Pegasus, 1968.

407 "A Symposium: Religion and Public Education." Religious Education 52 (July 1957): 247-306.

408 "Symposium: Religion and the Public Schools." Religious Education 61 (January 1966): 13-29.

409 "Symposium: Religion in the Public Schools." Religious Education 59 (November 1964): 443-79+.

410 Taft, Charles P. "Religion and the Public Schools." Christian Century 69 (August 20, 1952): 944-46.

411 Tanner, P. "Religious Education of Public School Pupils." The Catholic School Journal 38 (April 1938): 89-90.

412 Thayer, Vivian Trow. "Our Secular Schools and Religion."
     Phi Delta Kappan 34 (June 1953): 394-98.

413 ———. "Religion and the Public Schools." Harper's
     Magazine 188 (April 1944): 458-66.

414 ———. Religion in Public Education. New York: Viking,
     1947.

415 ———. "Religion in the Public Schools." Educational
     Administration and Supervision 34 (March 1948): 157-58.

416 Thimm, Fred. "The Need for Religious Education in
     American Public Schools." M.A. thesis. Wayne State
     University, 1957.

417 Till, Jacob E. "An Inquiry into Religious Values in
     the Public School Curriculum." M.A. thesis. Univer-
     sity of Omaha, 1957.

418 "Tracing the 'Wall': Religion in the Public School
     System." Yale Law Journal 57 (April 1948): 1114-22.

419 Trager, Frank N. "The Big Blooming Buzzing Confusion--
     Religion in Public Education." Religious Education
     46 (March-April 1951): 82-89.

420 ———. "The Relation of Religion to Public Education
     in America." Ph.D. dissertation. New York University,
     1951.

421 Trickey, Edna B. "A Public School Course Reveals God."
     International Journal of Religious Education 34
     (December 1957): 9-11.

422 Turner, A. C. "Shall the State Teach Religion?"
     Baptist Standard 56 (November 9, 1944): 1-2.

423 Tyack, David. "The Kingdom of God and the Common
     School." Harvard Educational Review 36 (Fall 1966):
     447-69.

424 Tydings, J. Mansir. "Kentucky Pioneers." Religious
     Education 51 (July-August 1956): 246-49.

425 ———. "Religion and the Public Schools; Kentucky
     Pioneers." Religious Education 51 (July 1956):
     246-49.

426 Tyree, Marshall J. "Should What is Rendered to God be Commanded by Caesar?" The Phi Delta Kappan 44 (November 1962): 74-76.

427 Vanden Berge, Harold O. "Religious Education in the Public Schools of South Dakota." M.A. thesis. University of South Dakota, 1947.

428 Van Dusen, Henry P. God in Education. New York: Scribners, 1951.

429 ————, and John K. Norton. "What Should be the Relation of Religion and Public Education?" Teachers College Record 56 (October 1954): 1-15.

430 Van Loon, Thomas. "Religion and Public Education." Adult Teacher (November 1955): 9-11.

431 Vars, G. F., and W. T. Lowe. "Social Forces Influencing Curriculum Decisions: Religion." Review of Educational Research 33 (June 1963): 255-56.

432 Vieth, Paul H. "The Function of the Public Schools in Dealing with Religion; Evaluation." Religious Education 48 (March 1953): 77-80.

433 Voss, Donald Henry. "The Relation of Religion to Public High School Education." M.S. thesis. Northern Illinois University, 1957.

434 Wallace, D. L. "Religion and the Public Schools." The Christian Century 83 (May 11, 1966): 612-15.

435 Walsh, Francis A. "Christianity in Public Schools." The American School Board Journal 93 (October 1936): 43.

436 ————. "Religion and Education." Commonweal 25 (January 15, 1937): 317-19.

437 Walsh, L. S. "Religious Education in the Public Schools of Massachusetts." American Catholic Quarterly 29 (January 1904): 93-118.

438 Weigle, Luther A. "The Crisis of Religion in Education; Schools Cannot be Neutral as to God." Vital Speeches 20 (December 15, 1953): 147-49.

439 Weigle, Luther A. "Public Education and Religion." Religious Education 35 (April-June 1940): 67-75.

440 ———. "The Relation of Church and State in Elementary Education." International Journal of Religious Education 5 (November 1928): 12-14.

441 ———. "Religion in Public Education." University of Pennsylvania Bulletin 42 (June 26, 1942): 340-52.

442 Wenner, George U. Religious Education and the Public School. Philadelphia: United Lutheran Publishing House, 1920.

443 "What Shall Public Schools Teach about Religion?" The School Executive 70 (December 1950): 57-66.

444 Whelan, Charles M. "Religion, Orthodoxy, Public Schools." America 108 (May 4, 1963): 640-43.

445 Wigmore, Ernest Charles. "The Place and Power of Religious Teaching in a Liberal Education." M.A. thesis. University of Oregon, 1913.

446 Williams, George Hunston. "Church-State Separation and Religion in the Schools of our Democracy." Religious Education 51 (September-October 1956): 369-77.

447 ———. "The Church, the Democratic State, and the Crisis in Religious Education." Harvard Divinity School Bulletin 46 (1949): 35-61.

448 Williams, H. V. "What Can Be Done, about Teaching Religion in the American Public School?" Nation's Schools 48 (September 1951): 64-66, 68.

449 Williams, John Paul. The New Education and Religion, A Challenge to Secularism in Education. New York: Association Press, 1945.

450 ———. Religious Education, Ignored but Basic to National Well-Being." School and Society 57 (May 22, 1943): 598-600.

451 ———. "The Schoolmen and Religion." School and Society 70 (August 13, 1949): 97-100.

452 Wilm, Emil Carl. Religion and the School. New York: The Abingdon Press, 1918.

453 Winchester, B. S., and H. M. Watts. "Shall We Force Religion Into the Schools?" Forum 77 (June 1927): 802-17.

454 Winter, Sister Teresa Elizabeth. "An Analysis of Religious Education for Public School Children with a Course of Study for the First Four Years on the Elementary School Level." M.A. thesis. St. John's University, 1942.

455 Withey, Raymond A. "A Neglected Area of Education." Educational Administration and Supervision 38 (February 1952): 76-82.

456 Wood, James E., Jr. "Religion and Education: A Continuing Dilemma." Annals of the American Academy of Political and Social Science 446 (November 1979): 63-77.

457 Woods, Ray Cleo. "The Status of Cooperation Between Church and Public School in Towns in Iowa under Five Thousand Population." M.A. thesis. University of Iowa, 1924.

458 Worrell, Edward K. Restoring God to Education. Wheaton, Illinois: Van Kampen Press, 1950.

459 Worth, Charles L. "The Public Schools and Religious Education." School and Society 52 (September 28, 1940): 252-56.

460 Wright, H. A. "Religion in the Schools." Educational Review 72 (June 1926): 46-52.

461 Yeaxlee, B. A. "Religion in the Schools." Religious Education 61 (March 1961): 118-124.

462 Zwierlein, Frederick J. "Opposition to Religious Education in Public Schools." Social Justice Review 41 (July-August 1948): 114-17; (September 1948): 149-52.

CHAPTER 2
MORAL EDUCATION

An attempted alternative to the religious strife and antagonism that often occurred when schools tried to provide religious instruction is explored in this chapter. Educators and religion specialists promoted the concepts of "moral education," "character training," "the whole man." During World War II religion was regarded as an essential underpinning of democracy. By the 1970s "values education" was frequently discussed as a way of meeting the objections that today's public education is valueless.

Promoters of this rather vague concept presupposed that a consensus exists in U.S. society regarding essential and fundamental values. And this consensus was held to be related to Judeo-Christian presuppositions. When reading these selections, note the chronological and era changes. American values have undergone significant development.

463 Allison, C. W. "What Spiritual Values should be Included in the Secondary School Program?" National Association of Secondary School Principals Bulletin 33 (May 1949): 83-88.

464 Allport, Gordon W. "Values and Our Youth." Teachers College Record 63 (December 1961): 211-19.

465 Amatora, S. M. "Educate the Whole Child." Education 71 (February 1951): 393-96.

466 Ammerman, K. G. "As Children View Religious Education." Childhood Education 19 (April 1943): 344-48.

467 Anderson, Paul S. "A Code of Moral and Spiritual Values." The Educational Forum 20 (May 1956): 401-06.

468 Axelrod, Joseph. "The Public Educator's Dilemma in the Communication of Values." Religious Education 49 (September 1954): 325-32.

469 Barden, Carrie. "Direct Moral Education: An Experiment." Education 42 (January 1922): 296-304.

470 Barnes, John B. "Can We Teach Silently?" The Educational Forum 22 (March 1958): 289-91.

471 Bartlett, Edward R. "Teaching Religion in a Democracy." Teachers College Journal 15 (January 1944): 70-71.

472 Battrick, Delmar H. "Moral and Spiritual Values in the Public Schools." Midland Schools 66 (December 1951): 15-16.

473 ———, and Giles Theilmann. "How Are Schools Including Moral and Spiritual Values in the School Program?" National Association of Secondary School Principals Bulletin 39 (April 1955): 141-46.

474 Beck, Robert H. "Religion and Spiritual Values in Public Education." School and Society 67 (March 27, 1948): 229-32.

475 Berns, Walter. "Will the Public School Movement for Character Education Supersede the Church School?" Religious Education 23 (May 1928): 462-65.

476 Blackston, Helen G. "Moral and Spiritual Vales in Public Education: Primary Grades." M.A. thesis. University of Texas, 1954.

477 Blakeman, Edward W. "When We Interpret Values: First Steps Toward Successful Teaching of Religious Values in the Classroom." Nation's Schools 48 (October 1951): 38-41.

478 Bortner, Ross L. "Teaching Spiritual Values in the Elementary Public School." Ph.D. dissertation. University of Pennsylvania, 1956.

479 Bouton, Eugene. "Moral Training in Schools." Education 8 (March 1888): 411-21.

480 Bower, William Clayton. Moral and Spiritual Values in Education. Lexington, Kentucky: University of Kentucky Press, 1952.

481 ———. "Trends in Moral and Spiritual Values in the Public Schools." Religious Education 48 (January-February 1953): 22-25.

482 Breig, Joseph A. "Lest They Know Not God." America
105 (August 12, 1961): 608-10.

483 Bremeld, Theodore, and Stanley Elam. Values in American
Education. Bloomington, Indiana: Phi Delta Kappan,
Inc., 1964.

484 Broudy, Harry S. "Religious Literacy and the American
School." Religious Education 48 (November 1953):
384-88.

485 Brouillette, Eloise Norma. "Moral and Spiritual Values
in Health Education." M.S. thesis. University of
California (Los Angeles), 1960.

486 Brubacher, John S., ed. The Public Schools and Spirit-
tual Values. New York: Harper and Row, 1944.

487 ————. "The Public Schools and the Crisis in Spirit-
tual Values." New York State Education 33 (April
1946): 531-34.

488 ————. "Why Force Religious Education?" Nation's
Schools 36 (November 1945): 23-24.

489 Cabot, Ella Lyman. "An Unsectarian Religion for Our
Schools." Religious Education 19 (February 1924):
39-44.

490 Carpenter, William Weston, and W. E. Drake. "Religion
and Education in the Frame of Democratic Government."
School and Society 55 (May 9, 1942): 530-32.

491 Carr, William G. "How Can We Teach Moral and Spiritual
Values in the Public Schools?" Religious Education
56 (July 1951): 195-98.

492 Chace, Elizabeth B. "The Teaching of Morality in
Schools." Education 4 (September 1883): 15-24.

493 Childs, John L. "Spiritual Values in Public Education."
Teachers College Record 48 (March 1947): 367-73.

494 Clifford, J. "Towards Educational Righteousness."
Nineteenth Century 68 (October 1910): 632-46.

495 Coe, George A. "Religion, Education, Democracy."
Religious Education 35 (July-September 1940): 131-37.

496 Coe, George A. "Shall the State Teach Religion?"
     School and Society 51 (February 3, 1940): 129-33.

497 ———. "The Religious Spirit in the Secondary School."
     The School Review 13 (October 1905): 581-96.

498 Courter, Claude V. "Teaching of Moral and Spiritual
     Values in the Cincinnati Public Schools." Religious
     Education 51 (July 1956): 271-72.

499 Cowley, Arthur Ernest. "The Religious Education of the
     Boy in Senior High School." Ph.D. dissertation.
     Southern Baptist Theological Seminary, 1931.

500 Dana, Ellis H. "Education for What?" Christian Educa-
     tion 30 (December 1947): 323-39.

501 Davis, Jesse B. "Moral Training and Instruction in
     High Schools." Religious Education 11 (October
     1916): 394-402.

502 Davis, Robert Clarence. "Character Education in the
     Public Schools." S.T.M. thesis. Theological Semi-
     nary (Philadelphia), 1938.

503 Dawson, Eugene E. "Do Schools Teach Values?" Inter-
     national Journal of Religious Education 42 (September
     1965): 20-21.

504 Delany, Shelden P. "Morality and the Public Schools."
     Education 28 (October 1907): 97-112.

505 Department of Elementary School Principals. Spiritual
     Values in the Elementary School. Washington, D.C.:
     National Education Association, 1947.

506 Dunigan, David R. "Modern American Systems of Character
     Education." The Catholic Educational Review 39 (May
     1941): 265-75.

507 Edmondson, J. B. "Do the Public Schools Emphasize
     Moral and Spiritual Values?" Kentucky School Journal
     32 (December 1953): 10-12.

508 ———. "Moral and Spiritual Values in Public Educa-
     tion." Michigan Education Journal (February 1953):
     322-24.

509 Educational Policies Commission. <u>Moral and Spiritual</u>
     <u>Values in the Public Schools.</u> Washington, D.C.:
     National Education Association, 1951.

510 Ellis, Samuel R. "Moral Education in a Democracy."
     <u>Education</u> 50 (March 1930): 407-13.

511 Emme, Earle E. "New Iowa Plan of Character Education."
     <u>The Phi Delta Kappan</u> 20 (December 1937): 124-27+.

512 Fadenrecht, John H. "Moral and Spiritual Values in
     Public Education." <u>Educational Administration and</u>
     <u>Supervision</u> 43 (January 1957): 49-58.

513 Fahs, Sophia Lyons. "Religion in the Public Schools--
     Values at Stake." <u>Childhood Education</u> 18 (February
     1942): 245-51.

514 Falconer, David Edwin. "A Study of the Teaching of
     Moral and Spiritual Values in Selected Public Schools
     of East Tennessee." M.S. thesis. University of
     Tennessee, 1954.

515 Flett, Hazel, and Alice Pittman. "The Public School
     Builds Moral Character." <u>Progressive Education</u> 26
     (February 1949): 118-20.

516 Flynn, Luther. "A Study of Moral, Spiritual, and
     Religious Values in the Public Schools of Virginia."
     Ed.D. dissertation. University of Virginia, 1956.

517 Fosdick, Harry E. "Our Religious Illiterates."
     <u>Reader's Digest</u> 54 (February 1949): 97-100.

518 ------. "Shall American School Children be Religiously
     Illiterate?" <u>School and Society</u> 66 (November 29,
     1947): 401-06.

519 Friedman, Edgar Z. "New Value Conflicts in American
     Education." <u>School Review</u> 74 (Spring 1966): 66-94.

520 Froula, V. K. "The Morals and Moral Training of High-
     School Students." <u>The School Review</u> 22 (November
     1914): 620-33.

521 Futrall, Emily. "A Historical Study of Religious and
     Moral Training in Public Schools of the United States."
     M.A. thesis. Tulane University, 1927.

522   Gates, Thomas S. "Spiritual and Moral Values." <u>School</u>
      <u>and Society</u> 69 (April 16, 1949): 273-76.

523   Goldin, Judah. "Public Education and Spiritual Values."
      <u>Religious Education</u> 48 (March 1953): 81-84.

524   Golightly, Thomas J. "The Present Interest in Character
      Education." <u>The Phi Delta Kappan</u> 9 (April 1927):
      140-44.

525   Hall, Charles C. "Progress in Religious and Moral
      Education." <u>Educational Review</u> 28 (June 1904):
      1-18.

526   Hall, George V., and Thomas E. Walt. "Spiritual Values
      Can be Taught." <u>The Nation's Schools</u> 60 (August
      1957): 39-41.

527   Haney, Eleanor Humes. "The Moral Life and Public
      Education." <u>Religious Education</u> 60 (November 1965):
      467-72.

528   Harrell, Mary Adelia. "A Study of the Development of
      Moral and Spiritual Values in a Seventh Grade Class."
      M.A. thesis. University of Florida, 1955.

529   Hartford, Ellis Ford. <u>Emphasizing Moral and Spiritual</u>
      <u>Values in a Kentucky High School</u>. Lexington,
      Kentucky: University of Kentucky, 1952.

530   ———. <u>Emphasizing Values in Five Kentucky Schools</u>.
      Lexington, Kentucky: University of Kentucky, 1954.

531   ———. <u>Moral Values in Public Education; Lessons from</u>
      <u>the Kentucky Experience</u>. New York: Harper and Row,
      1958.

532   Henkes, Robert. "Moral and Spiritual Values Through
      Art." <u>School Arts</u> 58 (October 1958): 27-30.

533   Hervey, Walter L. "Moral Education in the Public
      Elementary Schools." <u>Religious Education</u> 2 (August
      1907): 81-85.

534   ———. "Religious and Moral Teaching in the School."
      <u>Outlook</u> 82 (February 10, 1906): 316-20.

535 Holtz, Adrian Augustus. "A Study of the Moral and
    Religious Elements in American Secondary Education
    up to 1800." Ph.D. dissertation. University of
    Chicago, 1914.

536 Hook, Sidney. "Moral Values and/or Religion in Our
    Schools." Progressive Education 23 (May 1946):
    256-57+.

537 Horne, Herman H. "Moral and Religious Instruction in
    the Public Schools." Virginia Journal of Education
    17 (March 1924): 269-71.

538 ———. "A Program for the Religious Education of a
    Community." International Journal of Religious
    Education 5 (October 1928): 13-14.

539 "How Can We Teach Moral and Spiritual Values? Illinois
    Education Association Committee on Moral and Spiritual
    Values." Illinois Education 40 (1951): 122-25; 40
    (March 1952): 260-61.

540 Howland, George. "Moral Training in our Public Schools."
    Education 1 (November 1880): 144-55.

541 Hunter, David R. "Complete Education Includes Religion."
    International Journal of Religious Education 40
    (June 1964): 8-9.

542 Imbler, Ray Malcolm. "The Teaching of Moral and Spirit-
    ual Values in California Public Schools." Ed.D.
    dissertation. Stanford University, 1954.

543 Insko, W. R. "Moral and Spiritual Values in Education."
    Kentucky School Journal 30 (December 1951): 19-21.

544 Janet, Sister Mary, and Ralph G. Chamberlin. "What Are
    We Doing about Spiritual Values and Character Educa-
    tion for Present-Day Youth?" The National Association
    of Secondary School Principals Bulletin 40 (April
    1956): 252-56.

545 Janove, E. B. "Moral and Spiritual Values." Illinois
    Education 53 (March 1965): 305-08.

546 Jeffreys, M. V. C. "Confusion of Values and the
    Teacher's Responsibility." The Educational Forum
    25 (March 1961): 369-79.

547 Jewett, James P. "Moral Education in American Public
     Schools, 1800-1860." Ph.D. dissertation. University
     of Chicago, 1950.

548 Johnson, F. Ernest. "Education and Spiritual Values."
     Teachers College Record 48 (March 1947): 374-83.

549 ———. "Spiritual Values in the Secondary School."
     The National Association of Secondary School Princi-
     pals Bulletin 35 (April 1951): 47-52.

550 Jones, Olga. "Lasting Lessons in Spiritual Values."
     The National Parent Teacher 51 (April 1957): 18-20.

551 Kandel, I. L. "Character Formation: A Historical Per-
     spective." The Educational Forum 25 (March 1961):
     307-16.

552 Kilgore, W. J. "Public Schools and Moral Education:
     A Review Article." Journal of Church and State 2
     (May 1960): 37-43.

553 LaViness, Ruth A. "Teacher Looks at Influences on the
     Moral and Spiritual Development of Public School
     Children." M.Ed. thesis. University of Buffalo,
     1951.

554 Leavell, Ullin W. "On Teaching Spiritual Values."
     The Phi Delta Kappan 27 (December 1945): 99-102.

555 Ledden, W. E. "Spiritual Values and Public Education."
     New York State Education 33 (April 1946): 529-30.

556 Locke, Edward. "The Teaching of Morality in the Public
     School." The High School Journal 42 (November 1958):
     49-53.

557 Lum, Cheong, Olo Kagehiro, and Edwin Larm. "Some
     thoughts on Moral and Spiritual Values and the Secu-
     lar Public School." Progressive Education 30 (April
     1953): 166-71.

558 Mason, Robert E. Moral Values and Secular Education.
     New York: Columbia University Press, 1950.

559 ———. "Teaching Moral and Spiritual Values in the
     Public Schools: The Philosophical Issues." School-
     men's Week University of Pennsylvania Proccedings 52
     (1964): 45-58.

560 Maxson, William E. "The Administration of Moral Educa-
       tion in the Public Secondary School." M.A. thesis.
       Tufts College, 1953.

561 McCluskey, Neil G. Public Schools and Moral Education.
       New York: Columbia University Press, 1958.

562 ————. "Spiritual Values in the Public Schools."
       America 95 (September 29, 1956): 619-20.

563 McConnell, J. H. "Emphasis on the Spiritual." North
       Carolina Education 31 (March 1965): 28-29.

564 McFeely, Richard H. "Spiritual Values for Youth."
       Progressive Education 29 (November 1951): 51-56.

565 McGrath, G. D. "The Importance of Character and Moral
       Education in Teacher Training." Education 72
       (January 1952): 298-301.

566 Mead, Gertrude F. "The Teaching of Moral and Spiritual
       Values." M.A. thesis. Western Illinois State College
       (Macomb), 1955.

567 Medina, Harold R. "Public Education and Spiritual
       Values." Teachers College Record 56 (January 1955):
       203-06.

568 Michaelsen, Robert. "Moral and Spiritual Values Re-
       visited." Religious Education 62 (July 1967): 4-5.

569 Mills, John Delos. "A Study of Some Aspects of the
       Relation of Religious Education to Moral Character."
       M.A. thesis. University of Kansas, 1929.

570 Mones, Leon. "The Problem of Religious and Moral Educa-
       tion in our Public Schools." Education 74 (December
       1953): 250-56.

571 "Moral Instruction in Public Schools." Education 2
       (January 1882): 253-57.

572 "Moral and Spiritual Values." National Education Asso-
       ciation Research Bulletin 35 (December 1957): 168-71.

573 "Moral and Spiritual Values in the Public Schools--A
       Symposium." Religious Education 56 (July 1951):
       195-250.

574   Morgan, Joy Elmer. "Moral and Spiritual Values in the
      Public Schools." The National Elementary Principal
      31 (October 1951): 52-54.

575   Mowry, William A., et al. "Moral Education in Schools."
      Education 4 (September 1883): 1-14.

576   Moyer, James Wilson. "Religious Instruction and Char-
      acter Education in our Public Schools." B.D. thesis.
      Lancaster Theological Seminary, 1935.

577   Neff, Frederick C. "How Moral is Secular Education?"
      The Christian Century 73 (November 14, 1956): 1323-25.

578   Neumann, Henry. "Moral and Spiritual Values." Journal
      of Educational Sociology 30 (April 1957): 367-69.

579   Newcomb, R. S. "Introducing Moral and Religious Instruc-
      tion in the Public School." Elementary School Journal
      26 (June 1926): 782-86.

580   Norton, Edward J. "A Critical Analysis of Plans for
      Teaching Moral and Spiritual Values in Public Schools."
      M.A. thesis. The Catholic University of America, 1954.

581   Norton, Susan W. "Moral Education in the Public
      Schools." Education 42 (March 1922): 408-13; (April
      1922): 464-72; (June 1922): 615-21.

582   Parson, Howard L. "The Ground for Moral and Spiritual
      Values." Teachers College Record 55 (October 1953):
      24-36.

583   Payne, Elizabeth Caraman. "Moses is Nobody." Christian
      Century 68 (January 24, 1951): 106-08.

584   Pixley, Erma E. "Brief Sketch of the Development of
      Moral and Spiritual Values in the Los Angeles City
      Schools." Religious Education 51 (July 1956): 272-75.

585   Price, Lewis V. "Moral Education." Education 16
      (September 1895): 1-7.

586   Prince, John T. "Moral Training in the Public Schools."
      Education 33 (October 1912): 65-70; (November 1912):
      138-43.

587 Raths, Louis E., Merrill Harmin, and Sidney B. Simon. Values and Teaching: Working with Values in the Classroom. Columbus, Ohio: Charles E. Merrill Books, 1966.

588 Ritts, Joe. "A Guide to Moral and Spiritual Values in the Elementary School." M.A. thesis. San Francisco State College, 1955.

589 Ruch, Thomas O. "Teaching Moral and Spiritual Values: A Study of Administrative Attitudes in the Public High Schools of California." M.A. thesis. Fresno State College, 1956.

590 Sargent, Edward Haynes. "Religious Knowledge of High School Seniors--Specific Facts Known Concerning Catholicism, Judaism, and Protestantism as Revealed by Tests in the Ithaca High School in the Year 1951-1952." Ph.D. dissertation. Cornell University, 1954.

591 Seiferth, Berniece. "Religion and Morality." Educational Horizons 47 (Spring 1969): 99-108.

592 Sjorgren, Douglass D. "The Teaching of Moral and Spiritual Values in Ninety-Six Nebraska High Schools." M.A. thesis. Nebraska State Teachers College (Kearney), 1958.

593 Slattery, John T. "Moral Education of Public School Children." M.A. thesis. State University of New York (Albany), 1916.

594 Smith, Henry Lester. Character Development Through Religious and Moral Education in the Public Schools of the United States. Bloomington: Bureau of Cooperative Research, Indiana University, 1937.

595 Smith, Herbert F. A. "Teaching Spiritual Values in the Public Schools." Religious Education 50 (July 1955): 243-46.

596 Spangler, George P. "The Legal Status of Moral and Religious Education in the Public Schools of the United States." M.S. thesis. Temple University, 1929.

597 Stahmer, H. "Religion and Moral Values in the Public Schools." Religious Education 61 (January 1966): 20-26.

598 Stearns, Alfred E. "Moral Standards in the Schools."
     Education 32 (May 1912): 529-38.

599 Stone, William Jack. "San Diego Schools Teach Spiritual
     Values." The Nation's Schools 44 (December 1949):
     30-32.

600 Taylor, Charles K. "Moral Education--the History of an
     Experiment." Education 35 (December 1914): 220-30.

601 "Teaching Religion in a Democracy: A Special Number
     Dealing with the Relations of Religious Education to
     Public Education." International Journal of Religious
     Education 17 (November 1940): 6-16.

602 Towns, Elmer Leon. "An Analysis of the Implications of
     Teaching Morals in the Public Schools." M.A. thesis.
     Southern Methodist University, 1958.

603 Trevitt, Virginia Stewart. "A Study of the Program of
     Moral and Spiritual Values in Education in the State
     of Kentucky." M.A. thesis. Claremont Graduate
     School, 1956.

604 Trow, William Clark. "Dr. Fosdick and Religious Illit-
     eracy." School and Society 67 (March 27, 1948):
     240-41.

605 ————. "How Shall We Teach Ethics?" The School
     Review 59 (December 1951): 519-23.

606 Tuttle, Harold. "Shall Moral Teaching be Camouflaged?"
     Education 46 (April 1926): 469-75.

607 Updegraph, C. Leslie. "Present Status of Moral Educa-
     tion in the Public Schools." The Phi Delta Kappan
     9 (April 1927): 137-40.

608 Voight, John J. "Moral and Spiritual Values in Public
     Education." Catholic Theological Society of America,
     Proceedings XII (1956): 92-114.

609 Warren, S. Edward. "Moral Instruction in Schools."
     Education 15 (January 1895): 297-305.

610 Waterman, Leroy. "Education Incomplete Without Reli-
     gion." The Nation's Schools 37 (April 1946): 31-32;
     37 (May 1946): 53-54.

611 White, E. E. "Moral Training in the Public School." <u>Education</u> 7 (December 1886): 223-33.

612 Whiteside, Thomas R. "Moral and Spiritual Values in the High Schools of Shelby County, Texas." M.A. thesis. Stephen F. Austin State College, 1953.

613 Wilson, John W. "What Spiritual Values Should be Included in the Secondary-School Program?" <u>National Association of Secondary School Principals Bulletin</u> 33 (May 1949): 71-82.

614 Wolcott, D. "Public Schools and Ecumenical Education." <u>Religious Education</u> 62 (March 1967): 192-195.

615 Wood, Virginia N. "Spiritual and Moral Education in the Public Schools Curriculum." Ph.D. dissertation. Stanford University, 1950.

616 Zipp, J. A. "Schools and Character Education." <u>Education</u> 83 (March 1963): 425-28.

CHAPTER 3
SCHOOL PRAYER: HISTORY

Some historical background may be helpful for those who
want to place the school prayer controversy in perspective.
Feldberg (621) shows how an entire city was brought to civil
disorder by the prayer and Bible issue in 1844. How the
schools gradually moved from a religious (generally evangelical
Protestant) emphasis to one which accommodated pluralism is
charted in Brown (618). Wood (628) is always excellent.

See also 78, 51, 73 and 801.

617 Brickman, William W. "Public and Religious Education
     as Copartners in the Formation of American Society,
     1875-1964." Religious Education 59 (July 1964):
     294-305.

618 Brown, Samuel Windsor. The Secularization of American
     Education. New York: Columbia University Press, 1912.
     (Reprint by New York: AMS Press, 1972).

619 Doyle, E. P. "Prayer in the School: A Junior High
     School Survey." Social Education 28 (January 1964):
     18-20.

620 Drinan, Robert F. "Prayer in the Public Schools."
     America 102 (October 17, 1959): 70-71.

621 Feldberg, Michael. The Philadelphia Riots of 1844.
     Westport: Greenwood Press, 1975.

622 Healey, Robert M. Jefferson on Religion in Public
     Education. New Haven: Yale University Press, 1962.

623 Levy, L. W. "School Prayers and the Founding Fathers."
     Commentary 34 (September 1962): 225-30.

624 McDonald, Julius Flake. "The Influence of Religion on
     American Education During the Colonial Period."
     M.A. thesis. University of Chicago, 1910.

625 Menendez, Albert J. "School Prayer Can Hurt." Church
     and State 35 (September 1982): 15-18.

626 Sky, T. "Establishment Clause, the Congress and the
     Schools: An Historical Perspective." Virginia Law
     Review 52 (December 1966): 1395 ff.

627 Sternberg, Irma O. "The Jeffersonian Tradition in
     Regard to Religion in Public Education." M.A. thesis.
     Memphis State University, 1954.

628 Wood, James E., Jr. "Religion and Public Education in
     Historical Perspective." Journal of Church and State
     14 (Autumn 1972): 397-414.

CHAPTER 4
SCHOOL PRAYER IN THE COURTS

The landmark Supreme Court decisions against mandated
school prayer and Bible readings as devotional exercises in
public schools in the early 1960s (<u>Engel v. Vitale</u> and
<u>Abington v. Schempp</u>) were widely discussed. Educational jour-
nals and religious publications expaticated and declaimed on
the ramifications of these epochal rulings for months after-
ward. A representative selection are included in this chapter.

Courts in the states had also been called upon to unravel
the legal problems of religious devotions and readings in tax-
supported schools. Some of these decisions go back to the
19th century. Legal analyses are also included in chapter 4,
except those dealing specifically with Bible-reading, which
can be found in chapter 8. For additional legal perspectives
see the following: 68, 299, 868, 894, 915, 956, 891-893, 976,
1061, 1084, 1091, 1094, 1103, 1151, 1162, 1168, 1171, 1179,
1190, 1194, 1207, 1227, 1277, 1298, 1328, 1343, 1360, 1369,
1546-1549, 1554, 1556.

629 Austin, Orval Henry. "The Legal Status of Bible Read-
     ing and Other Religious Influences in the Public
     Schools of the United States." M.A. thesis. Univer-
     sity of Iowa, 1932.

630 Ball, William B. "The School Prayer Case." <u>Catholic
     Lawyer</u> 8 (Summer-Autumn 1962): 286 ff.

631 ———, and William J. Kenealy. "Proposed Prayer and
     Bible Reading Amendments: Contrasting Views."
     <u>Catholic Lawyer</u> 10 (Summer 1964): 185 ff.

632 ———. "The Forbidden Prayer." <u>Commonweal</u> 76 (July
     27, 1962): 419-22.

633 ———. "The Prayer Amendments: A Catholic Lawyer's
     View." <u>The Catholic World</u> 199 (September 1964):
     345-51.

634 Bedsole, Adolph. The Supreme Court Decision on Bible Reading and Prayer: America's Black Letter Day. Grand Rapids: Baker, 1964.

635 Berns, Walter. "School Prayers and 'Religious Warfare.'" National Review 14 (April 23, 1963): 315-18.

636 Blanshard, Paul. "The Big Decision." The Humanist 23 (July 1963): 106-10.

637 Boehm, C. H. "Supreme Court Bible Decision Stirs Both Legal and Philosophical Discussions." Pennsylvania School Journal 112 (October 1963): 68-69.

638 Bozell, L. Brent. "Saving our Children from God." National Review 15 (July 16, 1963): 19-22+.

639 Brant, Irving. "Madison and the Prayer Case." New Republic 147 (July 30, 1962): 18-20.

640 Brickman, William W. "Bible Readings, Prayers, and Public Schools." School and Society 91 (October 5, 1963): 272.

641 Brown, Ernest J. "Quis Custodiet Ipsos Custodes?--The School Prayer Cases." Supreme Court Review (1963): 1-33.

642 Butler, William J. "Regents Prayer Case: In the Establishment Clause, 'No Means No.'" American Bar Association Journal 49 (May 1963): 444 ff.

643 ————, and James A. Pike. "Has the Supreme Court Outlawed Religious Observance in the Schools?" Reader's Digest 81 (October 1962): 78-85.

644 Cahn, Edmond. "On Government and Prayer." New York University Law Review 37 (December 1962): 981 ff.

645 Calhoun, P. "School Prayer in Short Perspective." Connecticut Bar Journal 38 (December 1964): 643 ff.

646 Choper, Jesse H. "Religion in the Public Schools: A Proposed Constitutional Standard." Minnesota Law Review 47 (January 1963): 329-416.

647 "Church and State in American Education." Illinois Law Review 43 (July-August 1948): 374-88.

648 "Church and State: Prayer in Public Schools." Marquette Law Review 46 (Fall 1962): 233 f.

649 "The Churches and the Public Schools: A Policy Statement of the National Council of Churches." Journal of Church and State 5 (November 1963): 176-80.

650 Cogley, John. "Prayer and the Court." Commonweal 76 (August 10, 1962): 447-48.

651 "Constitutional Law--Religion in the Public Schools." Michigan Law Review 34 (June 1936): 1237-39.

652 "The Controversy Over the U.S. Supreme Court's 'School Prayer' Decisions: Pro and Con." Congressional Digest 43 (November 1964): 257-288.

653 Costanzo, Joseph F. "Prayer in Public Schools." Catholic Lawyer 2 (Autumn 1962): 269 ff.

654 ————. "Wholesome Neutrality: Law and Education." North Dakota Law Review 43 (Summer 1967): 605 ff.

655 "Court Bars Bible Reading in Public School." The Christian Century 79 (February 21, 1962): 220-21.

656 "Court Bars Lord's Prayer, Bible Reading in Schools." Congressional Quarterly Weekly Report 21 (June 21, 1963): 1001-02.

657 "The Court Decision--and the School Prayer Furor." Newsweek 60 (July 9, 1962): 43-45.

658 "The Court Decision on the Bible in Public School Libraries." School and Society 19 (February 9, 1924): 155.

659 "Court Decision on Bible Reading in Public Schools." The Catholic World 144 (March 1937): 750-51.

660 "The Court on Prayer." Commonweal 76 (July 13, 1962): 387-88; 78 (July 5, 1963): 388-89.

661 "Courts Bar Lord's Prayer, Bible Reading in Schools." Congressional Quarterly Weekly Report 21 (June 21, 1963): 1001-02.

662 Cusack, L. X. "Prayer Case--First Amendment Revision." Catholic Lawyer 8 (Autumn 1962): 281 ff.

663   Cushman, Robert Fairchild. "Public Support of Reli-
      gious Education in American Constitutional Law."
      Illinois Law Review 45 (1950-1951): 333-56.

664   ———. "Public Support of Religious Education in
      American Constitutional Law." Ph.D. dissertation.
      Cornell University, 1949.

665   Dalin, Galen E. "Some Legal Aspects of Religion in
      Public Schools of the United States." M.A. thesis.
      Minnesota State Teachers College. 1956.

666   Delahanty, William J. "Legal Aspects of Religious
      Education in Public Schools." M.A. thesis. State
      University of New York (Albany), 1932.

667   Dierenfield, Richard. "Impact of the Supreme Court
      Decisions on Religion in the Schools." Religious
      Education 62 (September 1967): 445-51.

668   Dixon, Robert G., Jr. "Religion, Schools, and the
      Open Society: A Socioconstitutional Issue." Jour-
      nal of Public Law 13 (1964): 267-309.

669   Doak, Edward Dale. "The Bible-Prayer Cases: Do Court
      Decisions Give Minority Rule?" Phi Delta Kappan 45
      (October 1963): 20-24.

670   Entry deleted.

671   ———. "The Legal Foundations of Religion and Public
      Education in the United States: Constitutional Pro-
      visions, Statutes, and Legal Interpretations in Each
      of Fifty States." Ed.D. dissertation. University
      of Colorado, 1963.

672   Dolbeare, Kenneth, and Phillip Hammond. The School
      Prayer Decisions. Chicago: University of Chicago,
      1971.

673   Donovan, John J. "Litigation Arising Out of Religious
      Questions Concerning the Common Schools." Ph.D.
      dissertation. University of Pittsburgh, 1937.

674   Drury, R. L., et al. "Religion in Public Schools:
      Educators and Religious Leaders Comment on the Signif-
      icance of the U.S. Supreme Court Decisions on Prayer
      in the Public Schools." Ohio Schools 42 (December
      1964): 12-20.

675 Duker, Sam. The Public Schools and Religion: The Legal
    Context. New York: Harper and Row, 1966.

676 Dukes, S. "The Supreme Court Ruling on School Prayer."
    The Educational Forum 27 (November 1962): 71-77.

677 Dykes, A. "Prayer and Bible Reading in the Schools."
    Tennessee Teacher 31 (November 1963): 12-14.

678 Engel, H. M. "School Prayer Issue, a Perverse Paradox."
    Catholic World 211 (June 1970): 125-27.

679 Fahy, Charles. "Religion, Education and the Supreme
    Court." Law and Contemporary Problems 14 (Winter
    1949): 73-91.

680 Farley, Andrew. "A Trilogy: Engel, Murray and Schempp:
    The Supreme Court and Public School Devotions."
    Union Seminary Quarterly Review 19 (November 1963):
    24+.

681 Fisher, Joseph A. "The Becker Amendment: A Constitu-
    tional Trojan Horse." Journal of Church and State 11
    (Autumn 1969): 427-55.

682 Fordham, Jefferson. "The Implications of the Supreme
    Court Decisions Dealing with Religious Practices in
    the Public Schools." Journal of Church and State 6
    (Winter 1964): 44-60.

683 Freeman, Thomas Jefferson. "The Opinions Expressed
    Toward the U.S. Supreme Court Decisions on Bible
    Reading and Prayer." Ph.D. dissertation. Auburn
    University, 1978.

684 Freund, Paul A., and Robert Ulich. Religion and the
    Public Schools: The Legal Issue; The Educational
    Issue. Cambridge: Harvard University Press, 1965.

685 Garber, Lee Orville. "Court Bars Bible Reading, but
    Finds Place for Religion in Schools." The Nation's
    Schools 72 (August 1963): 50-51.

686 ———. "Four Big Educational Issues Dominate Court
    Cases." The Nation's Schools (March 1964): 76-77.

687 ———. "Prayer Barred: What It Means." The Nation's
    Schools 70 (August 1962): 54+.

688   Garber, Lee Orville. "Religious Freedom is Limited."
      The Nation's Schools 75 (April 1965): 76.

689   ———. "Where Church-State Rulings Now Put Schools."
      The Nation's Schools 75 (June 1965): 42.

690   ———. "Where New Laws Chart New Routes for Public
      Schools." The Nation's Schools 79 (February 1967):
      114+.

691   Gauerke, Warren E. "Religion and the Public Schools:
      Some Legal Problems." School and Society 75 (June 28,
      1952): 401-04.

692   Glenn, John E. "Regents Prayer Decision: An Analysis
      of the Supreme Court Ruling." New York State Educa-
      tion 50 (October 1962): 20-21.

693   Greenberg, F. "To Pray or Not to Pray: Is That the
      Question?" PTA Magazine 63 (February 1964): 22-25+.

694   Griffiths, William E. "An Analysis of Judicial Deci-
      sions on Religion and the Public Schools." Ed.D.
      dissertation. University of Pennsylvania, 1963.

695   ———. Religion, the Courts and the Public ·Schools:
      A Century of Litigation. Cincinnati: W. H. Anderson
      and Company, 1966.

696   Hachten, William A. "Journalism and the Prayer Deci-
      sion." Columbia Journalism Review 1 (Fall 1962):
      4-9.

697   Hall, C. L. "Is Religion Banned From Our Schools?"
      Reader's Digest 86 (February 1965): 49-54.

698   Hamilton, Howard D. "God Banished From the Classroom
      Twice." Teachers College Journal 35 (March 1964):
      174-77.

699   ———. "God in the Classroom; the New York Regents
      Prayer Case." Social Science 38 (April 1963): 92-98.

700   Hanft, F. W. "Prayer Decisions." North Carolina Law
      Review 42 (April 1964): 567 ff.

701   Henle, Robert J. "Dilemmas of the Prayer Decision."
      Social Order 13 (March 1963): 32-48.

702 Holder, Angela Roddey. "Old Wine in New Bottles? The Right of Privacy and Future School Prayer Cases." Journal of Church and State 12 (Spring 1970): 289-307.

703 "How Would Founding Fathers Vote on School Prayer Case?" Michigan Education Journal 41 (December 1963): 12-13.

704 Hudgins, H. C., Jr., and R. A. Nelson. "Prayer, the Bible, and the Public Schools." The Education Digest 32 (December 1966): 22-25.

705 Hunt, Rolfe Lanier. "Policy Problems Arising from Current Trends and Recent Court Decisions." Religious Education 59 (July 1964): 313-21.

706 ———. "These Things Public Schools May Do." International Journal of Religious Education 42 (April 1966): 16-17.

707 Hyma, John, Jr. The Legal Basis of Relationships Between Religion and Education in the United States, 1945-1956. Ann Arbor: University of Michigan, 1959.

708 Iezzie, Anthony Joseph. "Public School Prayers and the Religion Clauses of the Constitution." Ph.D. dissertation. Case Western Reserve University, 1968.

709 Johnson, Alvin Walter. The Legal Status of Church-State Relationships in the U.S., with Reference to the Public Schools. Minneapolis: University of Minnesota Press, 1934.

710 Kahn, Journet. "Prayer and the Court." Commonweal 77 (November 30, 1962): 257-59.

711 Katz, E. "Patterns of Compliance With the Schempp Decision." Journal of Public Law 14 (1965): 396 ff.

712 Kauper, Paul G. "Prayer, Public Schools, and the Supreme Court." Michigan Law Review 61 (April 1963): 1031 ff.

713 Kean, C. D. "Reaction to Court Decision." The Christian Century 79 (July 18, 1962): 896-97.

714 Kenealy, W. J. "Prayer and Bible Reading in School Devotions." Religious Education 59 (July 1964): 327-329+.

715 Kik, Jacob Marcellus. <u>The Supreme Court and Prayer in the Public School</u>. Philadelphia: Presbyterian Reformed Publishing Company, 1963.

716 Kurland, Philip B. "The Regents' Prayer Case: 'Full of Sound and Fury, Signifying. . . .'" <u>Supreme Court Review</u> (1962): 1-33.

717 Langdon, Paul R. "New Laws or Decisions (Interpretation of U.S. Supreme Court's Decisions on Prayer)." <u>Ohio Schools</u> 42 (December 1964): 14-15.

718 LaNoue, G. R. "Supreme Court's New Frontier Between Religion and the Public Schools." <u>Phi Delta Kappan</u> 45 (December 1963): 123-27.

719 Lardner, L. A. "How Far Does the Constitution Separate Church and State?" <u>American Political Science Review</u> 45 (March 1951): 110-32.

720 Laubach, John H. <u>School Prayers: Congress, the Courts, and the Public</u>. Washington, D.C.: Public Affairs Press, 1969.

721 Leary, John P. "Prayer and the Supreme Court." <u>Thought</u> 37 (Winter 1962): 485-91.

722 "Legal Status of Religion in Indiana Common Schools." <u>Teachers College Journal</u> 22 (December 1950): 57-61.

723 Lindberg, Lucile, and Jeanette Veatch. "Supreme Court Decision on Religion in Public Schools." <u>The Instructor</u> 73 (October 1963): 43-44+.

724 Lipnick, Stanley M. "A New Trend in Civil Rights Litigation? Sunday Laws, Released Time, and Bible Reading in the Public Schools as Affected by the First Amendment." <u>George Washington Law Review</u> 28 (March 1960): 279-615.

725 "Local School Boards and Religion: The Scope of Permissible Action." <u>Santa Clara Lawyer</u> 6 (Fall 1965): 71 ff.

726 Lowry, Charles Wesley. <u>To Pray or Not to Pray!</u> Washington, D.C.: University Press of Washington, 1963.

727 Malone, Howard E. "A Review of the Laws Pertaining to Religion in the Public Schools of the United States." M.A. thesis. Claremont College, 1953.

728 Martin, William M. "Some Legal Aspects of Religion and the Public Schools." M.A. thesis. Morehead State College (Kentucky), 1952.

729 McCallum, James. "Supreme Court Decisions Concerning Religious Practices in the Public School Curriculum." M.S. thesis. Northern Illinois University, 1963.

730 Michaelsen, Robert. "The Supreme Court and Education in Religion." The Clearing House 39 (October 1964): 97-100.

731 Miller, E. O. "True Piety and the Regent's Prayer." Christian Century 79 (August 1, 1962): 934-36.

732 Miller, Raymond R. "The Legal Status of Religion in the Public Elementary and Secondary Schools of the United States." Ph.D. dissertation. Indiana University, 1949.

733 Mitchell, Frederic. "The Supreme Court of the United States on Religion and Education." Ph.D. dissertation. Teachers College, Columbic University, 1959.

734 Muir, William K. Prayer in the Public Schools. Chicago: University of Chicago, 1967. (New 1973 edition renamed Law and Attitude Change).

735 Nagel, Stuart, and Robert Erikson. "Editorial Reaction to Supreme Court Decisions on Church and State." Public Opinion Quarterly 30 (Winter 1966-1967): 647-55.

736 Niebuhr, Reinhold. "The Regents' Prayer Decision." Christianity and Crisis 22 (July 23, 1962): 125-26.

737 O'Brien, William. "Prayer, Public Schools and the Supreme Court." Michigan Law Review 61 (April 1963): 1031-86.

738 Patterson, Cecil H. "Religion in Education: Its Status Under Federal Law." Progressive Education 31 (October 1953): 22-25.

739   Peterson, Las, et al. "Law, Religion, and Public Educa-
      tion: Excerpts from Law and Public School Operation."
      School and Society 96 (December 7, 1968): 466-71.

740   Pfeffer, Leo. "Court, Constitution, and Prayer."
      Rutgers Law Review 16 (Summer 1962): 735 ff.

741   ———. "The Becker Amendment." Journal of Church and
      State 6 (Autumn 1964): 344-51.

742   ———. "The New York Regents' Prayer Case." Journal
      of Church and State 4 (November 1962): 150-58.

743   ———. "The Schempp-Murray Decision on School Prayers
      and Bible Reading." Journal of Church and State 5
      (November 1963): 165-175.

744   ———. "State-Sponsored Prayer." Commonweal 76
      (July 27, 1962): 417-19.

745   ———, and William B. Ball. "Religion and the Court."
      Commonweal 76 (July 27, 1962): 417-22.

746   Pleasants, S. A. "Schools and Religion: Court Rulings
      on the Bible and Prayer." The Clearing House 38
      (January 1964): 268-70.

747   Pollak, L. H. "Public Prayers in Public Schools."
      Harvard Law Review 77 (November 1963): 62-78.

748   Pollard, Marjorie Y. "The Legal Aspects of Teaching
      Religion in the Public Schools." M.A. thesis.
      Southwest State Teachers College (San Marcos, Texas),
      1957.

749   Powell, James O. "The School Prayer Battle." Saturday
      Review 46 (April 20, 1963): 62-64+.

750   Powell, T. "Conscience and the Constitution." PTA
      Magazine 58 (November 1963): 10-12.

751   Powers, Francis J. "Current Decisions on Religious
      Education and Observances in Public Schools." Cath-
      olic Educational Review 49 (April 1951): 217-27.

752   "Prayer in Our Public Schools." Florida Education 41
      (September 1963): 34-35.

753 "Prayer Still Legal in Public Schools." The Christian
    Century 79 (July 4, 1962): 832-33.

754 "Prayers, Bibles and Schools." The Christian Century
    79 (October 24, 1962): 1279-80.

755 Punke, Harold H. "Constitutional and Legal Aspects of
    the Church-State-School Problem." School and Society
    89 (May 6, 1961): 222-26.

756 Pusey, Merlo J. "The 'Wall' Between Church and State:
    United States Supreme Court's Decision in the School
    Prayer and Bible Reading Cases." New York State Bar
    Journal 37 (June 1965): 210-16.

757 Rainey, H. B. "Controversy Over School Prayer."
    National Association of Secondary School Principals
    Bulletin 48 (April 1964): 89-93.

758 Reich, D. R. "Supreme Court and Public Policy: The
    School Prayer Cases." Phi Delta Kappan 48 (September
    1966): 29-32.

759 "Religion and the Constitution--A Symposium on the
    Supreme Court Decisions on Prayer and Bible Reading
    in the Public Schools." Journal of Public Law 8
    (1964).

760 "Religion and the Constitution--A Symposium on the
    Supreme Court Decisions on Prayer and Bible Reading
    in the Public Schools." Journal of Public Law 13
    (1964): 245-503.

761 Rice, Charles E. "The Meaning of 'Religion' in the
    School Prayer Cases." American Bar Association
    Journal 50 (November 1964): 1047-60.

762 ———. The Supreme Court and Public Prayer. New York:
    Fordham University, 1964.

763 Rodes, Robert E., Jr. "The Passing of Nonsectarianism--
    Some Reflections on the School Prayer Case." Notre
    Dame Lawyer 38 (March 1963): 115-37.

764 Royse, Phillip Nicholas. "The Warren Court, the Estab-
    lishment of Religion and Schools." Ed.D. dissertation.
    University of Cincinnati, 1979.

765 "School Prayer--A Still Unsettled Controversy." Colum-
     bia Journal of Law and Social Problems 1 (June 1965):
     100 ff.

766 "School Prayer Ruling." Senior Scholastic 81 (September
     12, 1962): 24-26.

767 "School Prayers Decision." Senior Scholastic 83
     (September 13, 1963): 9-11.

768 "The Schools and Prayer." Newsweek 62 (September 9,
     1963): 82-83.

769 "Schools React to Court Decision." The Christian Cen-
     tury 80 (October 9, 1963): 1228-29.

770 "Schools--Reading the Bible and Reciting the Lord's
     Prayer as Violation of State Constitutional Provision
     Against Religious or Sectarian Instruction." Virginia
     Law Review 16 (March 1930): 509-10.

771 Schroeder, M. "Religious Education and State Laws."
     Lutheran Church Quarterly 3 (April 1930): 174-87.

772 Schumb, J. G., Jr. "Church, State and the Public
     Schools." Santa Clara Lawyer 4 (Fall 1963): 54 ff.

773 ------. "Religion in the Public Schools: Past and
     Future." Santa Clara Lawyer 3 (Spring 1963): 135 ff.

774 Schwartz, B. "Religion in Education: A Legal Perspec-
     tive." Teachers College Record 64 (February 1963):
     363-66.

775 Sheerin, John B. "Ban on Public School Prayer."
     Catholic World 195 (August 1962): 261-65.

776 ------. "Decision on the Lord's Prayer and Bible
     Reading." The Catholic World 197 (August 1963):
     276-79.

777 Starr, I. "Recent Supreme Court Decisions: Separation
     of Church and State." Social Education 26 (December
     1962): 439-44.

778 Steinhilber, August W. "The Supreme Court Decision on
     Government-Sponsored Prayer." School Life 44 (July
     1962): 8-9.

779 Steinhilber, August W. "The U.S. Supreme Court and Religion in the Schools." Theory Into Practice 4 (February 1965): 8-13.

780 "Supreme Court Bible Decision Stirs Both Legal and Philosophical Discussions: Official Opinion." Pennsylvania School Journal 112 (October 1963): 68.

781 "Supreme Court Decision on Bible Reading and Prayer Recitation." NEA Journal 52 (September 1963): 55-56.

782 "Supreme Court Decision on the Reading of Prayer in Schools." The Humanist 22 (July 1962): 107-13.

783 "The Supreme Court, the First Amendment, and Religion in the Public Schools; the Case, the Problems Remaining, the Interpretation of the Establishment Clause." Columbia Law Review 63 (January 1963): 73-97.

784 Sutherland, Arthur E., Jr. "Constitution, Churches and Schools." Religious Education 51 (January 1956): 64-70.

785 ———. "Establishment According to Engel." Harvard Law Review 76 (November 1962): 25-52.

786 ———. "Public Authority and Religious Education: A Brief Survey of Constitutional and Legal Limits." Religious Education 52 (July 1957): 256-64.

787 ———. "The Supreme Court and the Public School." Harvard Educational Review 24 (1954): 71-85.

788 "This Month's Feature: Congress and the School Prayer Decision." Congressional Digest 43 (November 1964): 257-88.

789 "Thou Shalt Not Pray." National Review 13 (July 31, 1962): 51-52.

790 Tieszen, D. W. "Legal Concepts Concerning Religious Influences in Public Education as Defined by State Courts of Last Resort." Teachers College Record 55 (November 1953): 61-69.

791 Torcaso, Roy R. "The Supreme Court Decision on Reading of Prayer in Schools." Humanist 22 (July 1962): 107-13.

792   Voelz, Stephen John. "The Legal Status of Religion in
      Iowa Public Schools." M.A. thesis. Loyola University
      (Chicago), 1965.

793   West, Ellis M. "The Supreme Court and Religious Liberty
      in the Public Schools." Journal of Church and State
      25 (Winter 1983): 87-112.

794   West, Thomas H. "The Legal Aspects of Religious Educa-
      tion on Released Time." Religious Education 44
      (November 1949): 327-31.

CHAPTER 5
SCHOOL PRAYER AND POLITICS

School prayer made front-page headlines in 1984 as the U.S. Senate voted on a constitutional amendment that would have "restored" the practice of state-sponsored group prayer in U.S. public school classrooms. The proposal fell 11 votes short of passage. Similar proposals had been rejected in 1966 and 1971.

The political dimension of this issue is explored admirably by 795, 799 and 806. Kendall was a brilliant if erratic conservative thinker who revealed why political conservatives saw school prayer and religion generally as admirable activities related to their quest for order and continuity. Entry 801 relates school prayer to the concept of an established Christian political order, a view popular a century ago. Charles Rice (808-810) is the classical Catholic conservative. See also his 761-762 selections. Shugrue's doctoral dissertation (816) is helpful.

This issue will remain politically divisive for years to come. After all, we have a President who thinks God has been "expelled" from public schools.

795   Adams, William C. "American Public Opinion in the 1960s on Two Church-State Issues." Journal of Church and State 17 (Autumn 1975): 477-94.

796   Adler, Morris. "The Church-State Issue: 1964." Jewish Frontier 31 (March 1964): 18-21.

797   Baker, John Henry. "Religion in Public Education: Some Problems in Political Sociology." Religious Education 62 (May 1967): 245-50+.

798   Beaney, William M., and Edward N. Beiser. "Prayer and Politics: The Impact of Engel and Schempp on the Political Process." Journal of Public Law 13 (1964): 475-503.

799   Birkby, Robert H. "The Supreme Court and the Bible
      Belt." Mid-West Journal of Political Science 10
      (August 1966): 304-19.

800   Canavan, Francis P. "Implications of the School Prayer
      and Bible Reading Decisions: The Welfare State."
      Journal of Public Law 13 (1964): 439-46.

801   Colwell, Stephen. The Position of Christianity in the
      United States in Its Relations with Our Political
      Institutions, and Specially with Reference to Reli-
      gious Instruction in the Public Schools. Philadel-
      phia: Lippincott, 1854.

802   Conn, Joseph L. "Reagan Backs Government Sponsored
      School Prayer." Church and State 35 (June 1982):
      3, 21-22.

803   Exton, E. "Reactions of Congress to the Ruling of
      School Prayer." The American School Board Journal
      145 (September 1962): 66-70.

804   "First Amendment Wins Test." Church and State 25
      (January 1972): 8-10.

805   "House Judiciary Committee Center of School Prayer
      Battle." Congressional Quarterly Weekly Report 22
      (May 1, 1964): 881-85.

806   Kendall, Willmoore. "American Conservatism and the
      'Prayer' Decisions." Modern Age 8 (Summer 1964):
      245-59.

807   "Outlook Dim for Dirksen's School Prayer Proposals."
      Congressional Quarterly Weekly Report 24 (July 29,
      1966): 1643-46.

808   Rice, Charles E. "Is a Prayer Amendment Coming?"
      National Review 17 (July 13, 1965): 597-99.

809   ————. "Let Us Pray--An Amendment to the Constitution."
      Catholic Lawyer 10 (Summer 1964): 178-84+.

810   ————. "Where are the Clergymen: No Support for
      Dirksen's Prayer Amendment for Fear of Losing Federal
      Aid." National Review 18 (August 23, 1966): 833-35.

811   "School Prayer Amendment: Political Football." Church
      and State 35 (September 1982): 10-11.

812 "School Prayer and the Becker Amendment." Georgetown Law Journal 53 (Fall 1964): 192 ff.

813 "School Prayer Controversy: Pro and Con." Congressional Digest 59 (December 1980): 289-314.

814 School Prayer: Hearings Before the Subcommittee on Constitutional Amendments of the Committee on the Judiciary, United States Senate. Washington, D.C.: U.S. Government Printing Office, 1966.

815 Seckinger, Richard K. "School Prayers and Bible Reading by Constitutional Amendment: An Analysis of 152 Congressional Proposals." Religious Education 60 (September 1965): 362-67.

816 Shugrue, Richard Edward. "Politics and Prayer: The Search for a National Consensus." Ph.D. dissertation. University of Nebraska, 1968.

817 Staff Study for the Committee on the Judiciary, House of Representatives. Proposed Amendments to the Constitution Relating to School Prayers, Bible Reading, Etc. (March 4, 1964).

818 Way, H. Frank, Jr. "Survey Research on Judicial Decisions: The Prayer and Bible Reading Cases." Western Political Quarterly 21 (June 1968): 189-205.

CHAPTER 6
SCHOOL PRAYER: PRO

Feelings on the school prayer issue are intense and always have been. Many of the items in Chapter 6 are expressions of viewpoints sympathetic to verbal, group prayer activities. Others favor full-scale inclusion of religious devotionals in public schools. Some see religious exercises as a way of maintaining continuity with our heritage. Perhaps the leading exponent of this view is noted by a constitutional lawyer William Ball (819-821).

See also 870, 871, 877, 882, 888, 914, 1470, and 1471 for additional expressions of sympathetic views.

819 Ball, William B. "Legal Religion in the Schools." Catholic World 197(September 1963): 366-71.

820 ———. "Of Schema, Hotheads, Theology and Smoke." Teachers College Record 64 (February 1963): 355-62.

821 ———. "Religious Liberty in Education." Journal of Ecumenical Studies 14 (Fall 1977): 667-71.

822 Brickman, William W. "Concept of Freedom in Education." The Educational Record 45 (Winter 1964): 74-83.

823 ———. "Religion and Education." School and Society 67 (March 27, 1948): 245-52.

824 ———. "Religious Education." School and Society 76 (October 25, 1952): 262-67.

825 Buchanan, G. Sidney. "Accommodation of Religion in the Public Schools." UCLA Law Review 28 (June 1981): 1000-1024.

826 Buddy, Charles F. "Bring the Ten Commandments Back into the Schools." America 93 (September 24, 1955): 613-15.

827   Cleary, Catherine B. "Putting God in a School System."
      America 85 (September 22, 1951): 595-96.

828   Dawson, Christopher. "Education and Christian Culture."
      Commonweal 59 (December 4, 1953): 216-20.

829   Fangmeir, Robert A. "For Restored Prayers." _The
      Christian Century_ 81 (January 1, 1964): 58-59.

830   Hagie, C. E. "Religion in the Schools?--Yes!" _School
      and Society_ 51 (May 25, 1940): 677-79.

831   McLean, M. D. "Our Religious Heritage and the Schools."
      Theory Into Practice 4 (February 1965): 1-2.

832   Warren, Rita. _Mom, They Won't Let Us Pray_. Waco: Word
      Books, 1975.

833   "We Must Permit Prayer in the Schools: School Admin-
      istrators Opinion Poll Findings." _The Nation's
      Schools_ 70 (September 1962): 101+.

CHAPTER 7
SCHOOL PRAYER: CON

Critics of formalized school prayer have not been silent. They have eloquently addressed the questions of religious liberty, freedom of conscience, religious tolerance and inter-faith harmony, believing that these principles are best pre-served when public schools maintain neutrality between reli-gious viewpoints.

Exponents of this persuasion range from humanists like Paul Blanshard (834) and John Dewey (839) to Methodists (837), Unitarians (838), Baptists (849), Episcopalians (847, 848), Jews (845) and Disciples of Christ (841). Those who have been persecuted by religious zealots and conformists see this issue in a particularly vivid light. See 835 (and 625).

834 Blanshard, Paul. "School Prayer Drive: Pious Lawless-ness." Church and State 32 (June 1979): 7-9.

835 Buie, Jim. "We Are Mothers Not Martyrs." Church and State 36 (November 1983): 4-5.

836 Corbett, J. Eliot. "Prayer in the Public Schools." Engage/Social Action 8 (December 1980): 6.

837 Courtis, Stuart A. "Religion Has No Place in Public Schools." Nation's Schools 39 (June 1947): 22-23.

838 Crooker, Joseph Henry. Religious Freedom in American Education. Boston: American Unitarian Association, 1903.

839 Dewey, John. "Religion and Our Schools." Hibbert Journal 6 (1908): 796-809.

840 Eisenberg, Arlene, and Howard Eisenberg. "Why Clergymen are Against School Prayer." Redbook 124 (January 1965): 38-39+.

841 Flowers, Ronald B. "Piety in Public Places." Christi-
     anity and Crisis 31 (November 1, 1971): 230-33.

842 Hill, Henry H. "Public Schools Must be Secular."
     Atlantic Monthly 190 (October 1952): 75-77.

843 Lewis, Joseph. "More Objections to Religion and the
     Bible in Public Schools." Teachers College Journal
     15 (January 1944): 52-53.

844 Morrill, True C. "Let's Keep Religion Out of the
     Schools." The Nation's Schools 37 (February 1946):
     46.

845 Newman, Louis. The Sectarian Invasion of Our Public
     Schools. San Francisco: 1925.

846 Travers, Edwin X. "The Pointlessness of School Prayer:
     A Teacher's View." Church and State 37 (September
     1980): 14-16.

847 Walker, Rev. John T. "The Place for Prayer." Washing-
     ton Diocese 53 (April 1984): 3.

848 White, Cecile Holmes. "Accidental Crusader." Church
     and State 36 (June 1983): 14-15.

849 Wood, James E., Jr. "Legislating Prayer in the Public
     Schools." Journal of Church and State 23 (Spring
     1981): 205-14.

CHAPTER 8

BIBLE READING

Classroom reading of the Bible has been a central conflict in American education because of the variety of translations, the sensitiveness toward controversial interpretation and the difficulty of achieving a consensus over how (or whether) the Book of Books should be included in the curriculum.

Court cases, emotional outbursts among the citizens, and carefully reasoned arguments have been written about this issue.

For example, conservative scholar C. John Miller (917) charges that all public school Bible courses are "naturalistic" and hostile to the view that the Scriptures possess "divine authority."

Intense community conflict often resulted from disputes over Bible reading (854, 894, 897, 911, 915, 916, 951). Religious conservatives have regarded it as essential to the educational process (865-66, 870-72, 877, 882, 885, 888). Many state courts ruled against daily Scripture lessons before the U.S. Supreme Court did so in 1963. (856, 868, 873, 876, 880, 881, 893, 899, 900, 908, 913, 920, 931, 948, 949, 952, 953, 956.)

850 Abbott, Lyman. "The Bible in the Schools." Current Literature 31 (July 1901): 9-10.

851 American Law Reports Annotated. "Bible Distribution or Reading in Public Schools." 45 ALR 2nd (1956): 742-74.

852 "The Bible and Religion in the Public Schools." Elementary School Journal 26 (September 1925): 4-6.

853 "The Bible in Public Schools." The Independent 54 (October 16, 1902): 2489-90.

854 The Bible in the Public Schools. Cincinnati: Robert
     Clarke and Company, 1870. (Reprint by New York:
     Da Capo Press, 1967).

855 "The Bible in the Public Schools of the State of
     Washington." School and Society 32 (August 31, 1930):
     284.

856 "Bible Out of the California Schools." Literary Digest
     75 (November 25, 1922): 33-34.

857 "Bible Reading and Prayer in Public Schools." Social
     Education 29 (October 1965): 361-71.

858 Entry deleted.

859 "Bible Reading and Prayer Recital in Public Schools."
     Maryland Law Review 20 (Winter 1960): 81 f.

860 "Bible Reading Decision Splits Administrators into Two
     Camps: School Administrators Opinion Poll." The
     Nation's Schools 72 (September 1963): 43.

861 "Bible Reading in Public Schools." Mississippi Law
     Journal 31 (March 1960): 169 f.

862 "Bible Reading in Public Schools." School and Society
     34 (November 7, 1931): 627-28.

863 "Bible Reading in the Public Schools." Michigan Law
     Review 58 (February 1960): 588 f.

864 "Bible Reading in the Public Schools." School and
     Society 16 (December 23, 1922): 715-16.

865 Black, Harold Garnet. "The Bible in American Schools."
     Christian Education 30 (December 1947): 314-22.

866 ———. "Shall We Break Another American Tradition?"
     Christian Education 28 (September 1944): 56-66.

867 Blackhurst, J. H. "Plea Against the Bible in the
     Schools." Education 43 (February 1923): 381-85.

868 Boyer, William W. "Bible in Wisconsin Public Schools:
     A Forbidden Book." Religious Education 55 (November
     1960): 403-09.

869 Bradshaw, L. A. "Bible Reading in the Public Schools."
    New Hampshire Bar Journal 7 (January 1965): 119 ff.

870 Cates, E. E. "Plea for the Bible in the Schools."
    Education 42 (June 1922): 611-14.

871 Cheever, George B. Right of the Bible in Our Public
    Schools. New York: Robert Carter and Brothers, 1854.

872 Clark, Rufus W. The Question of the Hour: The Bible
    and the School Fund. Boston: Lee and Shepard, 1870.

873 Coan, Robert J. "Bible Reading in the Public Schools."
    Albany Law Review 22 (January 1958): 156-73.

874 "Commission on Bible Study in Relation to Public Educa-
    tion." Religious Education 11 (October 1916): 455-58.

875 Consalvo, Gennaro J. "Bibles, Wall of Separation and
    Rationality." Catholic University of America Law
    Review 4 (May 1954): 118-27.

876 "Constitutional Law--Reading Bible in the Public
    Schools." Michigan Law Review 28 (February 1930):
    430-36.

877 Cook, Elizabeth B. The Nation's Book in the Nation's
    Schools. Chicago: The Chicago Woman's Educational
    Union, 1898.

878 "Courts and Bible Reading in the Public Schools." West
    Virginia Law Review 62 (June 1960): 353 ff.

879 "Courts Uphold Bible Reading, Congregational Autonomy."
    The Christian Century 69 (March 26, 1952): 356-57.

880 Creel, E. M. "Is it Legal for the Public Schools of
    Alabama to Provide an Elective Course in Non-Sectarian
    Bible Instruction?" The Alabama Lawyer 10 (January
    1949): 86-97.

881 Cushman, Robert Fairchild. "The Holy Bible and the
    Public Schools." Cornell Law Quarterly 40 (Spring
    1955): 475-99.

882 Dana, Richard Henry. The Bible in School. Boston:
    Massachusetts Sabbath School Society, 1855.

883 Dorey, Milnor. "Should Secondary Schools Teach the
     Bible?" The School Review 16 (December 1908): 680-82.

884 Douglas, William O. The Bible and the Schools. Boston:
     Little, Brown and Company, 1966.

885 Durant, Henry F. Defense of the Use of the Bible in the
     Public Schools. Boston: Ticknor and Fields, 1859.

886 Edington, Andrew H. "Bible Teaching Policies in the
     Public Schools." The Phi Delta Kappan 31 (April
     1950): 394-95.

887 Eisenberg, Emma-Louise. "Views of Representatives of
     Various Religious Faiths with Respect to the Place of
     The Bible in the Public Secondary School; Including a
     Summary of the Laws on the Subject and Some Represent-
     ative Plans for Bible Study Now Being Used in Cooper-
     ation with the Public Secondary Schools." M.A. thesis.
     Washington University (St. Louis), 1927.

888 Ellis, Samuel Moore. The Bible Indispensable in Educa-
     tion. Pittsburgh: National Reform Association, 1926.

889 Frommer, Arthur, ed. The Bible and the Public Schools.
     New York: Frommer, 1963.

890 Fry, Harrison W. "On Bible Reading in Schools." The
     Christian Century 79 (March 28, 1962): 408-09.

891 Garber, Lee Orville. "Bible Reading Upheld in Miami
     Public Schools." Nation's Schools 67 (June 1961):
     56-57, 88, 90.

892 ———. "Florida Bible Case Asks, 'Do Majorities have
     Rights, Too?'" Nation's Schools 70 (September 1962):
     110-11.

893 ———. "What the New Jersey Courts Say About Bible
     Reading in the Public Schools." Nation's Schools 50
     (July 1952): 61-62.

894 Geiger, John O. "The Edgerton Bible Case: Humphrey
     Desmond's Political Education of Wisconsin Catholics."
     Journal of Church and State 20 (Winter 1978): 13-28.

895 Harrison, Joseph W. "Bible, the Constitution and Public
     Education." Tennessee Law Review 29 (Spring 1962):
     363 ff.

896 Harrison, Joseph W. "The Bible, the Constitution and
     Public Eudcation: A Case Study of Religious Instruc-
     tion in the Public Schools of Knoxville and Knox
     County, Tennessee." M.A. thesis. University of
     Tennessee, 1961.

897 Helfman, Harold M. "The Cincinnati Bible War, 1869-
     1870." Ohio State Archaeological and Historical
     Quarterly 60 (October 1951): 369-86.

898 "High-School Bible Study in Virginia." Religious Educa-
     tion 13 (April 1918): 136-37.

899 Hood, William R. The Bible in the Public Schools,
     Legal Status and Current Practice. Washington, D.C.:
     U.S. Government Printing Office, 1923.

900 ————. "Bible in the Public Schools; Legal Status
     and Current Practice." U.S. Bureau of Education
     Bulletin 15 (1923): 1-13.

901 Horwill, Herbert W. "Bible in the Schools." Atlantic
     Monthly 92 (September 1903): 296-304.

902 Howard, W. G. "Florida Schools Ignore Ban on Bible
     Reading Survey Shows." The Nation's Schools 79
     (May 1967): 122.

903 Hunt, Mate Graye. "Bible Study and the Public Schools."
     Peabody Journal of Education 23 (November 1945):
     156-69.

904 Hurlbut, Elisha P. A Secular View of Religion in the
     State, and the Bible in the Public Schools. Albany,
     New York: J. Munsell, 1870.

905 Johnson, Alvin Walter. "Bible Reading in the Public
     School." Education 59 (January 1939): 274-80.

906 Johnston, Melvin Filmore. "A Study of the Legal Status
     of Bible Reading." M.A. thesis. University of
     Washington, 1931.

907 Jones, Alonzo T. The Place of the Bible in Education.
     Oakland: Pacific Press, 1903.

908 Keesecker, Ward W. Legal Status of Bible Reading and
     Religious Instruction in the Public Schools. Washing-
     ton, D.C.: U.S. Government Printing Office, 1930.

909   Kershner, George W. An Essay on State Schools and Religion; or, The Bible in the Public Schools. Princeton: Robinson and Company, 1881.

910   Knight, Ryland. "The Bible and the Public Schools." The Christian Index 128 (March 18, 1948): 10-23.

911   Lannie, Vincent P., and Bernard C. Diethron. "For the Honor and Glory of God: The Philadelphia Bible Riots of 1844." History of Education Quarterly 8 (Spring 1968): 44-106.

912   Lawrence, Augusta Jackson. "Bible in School." M.A. thesis. George Peabody College, 1920.

913   "Legal Status of Bible-Reading in Public Schools." School Review 39 (January 1931): 4-6.

914   Mayo, Amory Dwight. The Bible in the Public Schools. New York: J. W. Schermerhorn and Company, 1870.

915   McAtee, W. A. Must the Bible Go? A Review of the Edgerton Bible Case in Wisconsin. Madison: Tracy Gibbs, 1890.

916   Meyers, M. A. "The Children's Crusade: Philadelphia Catholics and the Public Schools, 1840-1844." Records of American Catholic Historical Society of Philadelphia 75 (1964): 103-27.

917   Miller, C. John. "Public School Bible Study: Sectarianism in Disguise." Christianity Today 13 (August 1, 1969): 3-5.

918   "Most Administrators Defend Bible Reading in Public Schools." Nation's Schools 66 (November 1960): 75.

919   Nygard, J. N. "Bible Reading Held Coercive. The Indiana Teacher and the Law." Indiana Teacher 108 (October 1963): 92-93.

920   Pearsall, Henry B. "Constitutional Law--Separation of Church and State; Bible Reading in the Public Schools." Michigan Law Review 58 (February 1960): 588-92.

921   Petrie, John Clarence, and Burdette E. Backus. "Shall We Teach the Bible in the Public Schools?" Teachers College Journal 15 (January 1944): 50-51, 56.

922 Poore, H. W. "The Study of Bible History in the Graded Schools." Education 16 (February 1896): 362-64.

923 Rainey, George S. Bibles in the Public Schools; or, a Plea for Religious Liberty. Otterbein, Indiana: 1924.

924 Rankin, John Alexander. "An Analysis of Biblical Selections Read in the Public Schools of Ligonier, Pennsylvania, During the School Year 1932-1933." M.A. thesis. University of Pittsburgh, 1933.

925 "Reading of the Bible in the Schools of New York." School and Society 42 (November 30, 1935): 734-35.

926 Rice, Arthur H. "It Can't Be Avoided: Bible Reading is an Act of Religion." The Nation's Schools 85 (September 1969): 26.

927 Rich, S. G. "What Portions of Scripture Shall We Use in the Schools?" Education 43 (October 1922): 93-98.

928 Roach, Stephen F. "Board Participation in Distribution of Bible." American School Board Journal 128 (April 1954): 37-38.

929 Roberts, Ernest F. "Bible Reading in Public Schools." America 102 (March 19, 1960): 737-38.

930 Ryan, Zelda Jeanne. "The Use of the Bible in Public Schools." Religion in Life 21 (Autumn 1952): 603-12.

931 Santee, Joseph Frederick. "The Legal Status of Public School Bible Reading." Social Studies 43 (November 1952): 291-93.

932 Schofield, Henry. "Religious Liberty and the Bill of Rights in the Illinois Public Schools." Illinois Law Review 6 (May 1911): 17-33; (June 1911): 91-111.

933 "Schoolmen Still Agonize Over Bible Reading Decision: School Administrators Opinion Poll." The Nation's Schools 80 (July 1967): 22.

934 Shepherd, W. G. "What is Wrong with the Bible?" Good Housekeeping 77 (December 1923): 28-29.

935 Shouse, J. B. "Appeal to Nature: An Item for High School Bible Study." The Educational Forum 21 (January 1957): 167-75.

936   Shriver, Mark O. "Reading the Bible in School."
      Commonweal 11 (November 27, 1929): 108-109.

937   Smith, Frederick E. "The Bible and Public Schools."
      The Christian Index 123 (July 29, 1943): 9-10.

938   Smythe, W. Herbert. The Bible and the Common Schools.
      Detroit: J. H. Caine and Company, 1870.

939   Snider, G. R. "Bible Reading and School Prayers: Some
      Guidelines." Phi Delta Kappan 48 (June 1967): 516-17.

940   Spear, Samuel Thayer. Religion and the State; or The
      Bible and the Public Schools. New York: Dodd, Mead
      and Company, 1876.

941   Squires, Vernon P. "The North Dakota Plan of Bible
      Study." Religious Education 11 (February 1916):
      20-24.

942   Steiner, Franklin. The Bible: Should it be in the
      School Room? The Question Considered Legally, Mor-
      ally, and Religiously. Girard, Kansas: Haldeman-
      Julius, 1924.

943   Steinhilber, A. W. "Bible Reading in the Public
      Schools." School Life 46 (October 1963): 13-16.

944   Straley, G. H. "How to Beat the Bible Ban." School
      Management 12 (March 1968): 65-66.

945   Tatsch, Rudolph Charles. "The Status of the Bible-for
      Credit Program in the Public High Schools of Texas."
      B.D. thesis. Texas Christian University, 1945.

946   "Teaching the Bible in Public Schools of America."
      Vision 11 (June 1965): 8-12.

947   Thomas, Issac. "Bible as a Textbook in the Public
      High Schools." The School Review 17 (December 1909):
      705-12.

948   Tiffany, Orrin E. "State Laws Relative to the Use of
      the Bible in or by the Public Schools." Religious
      Education 21 (February 1926): 76-80.

949   Torpey, William George. "Reading the Bible in Public
      Schools." in Judicial Doctrines of Religious Rights
      in America. Chapel Hill, North Carolina: University
      of North Carolina Press, 1948.

950 Torrey, Elizabeth C. "Bible in Texas High Schools."
     <u>International Journal of Religious Education</u> 23
     (January 1947): 13-14.

951 Treacy, Gerald C. "Father John Bapst and the Ellsworth
     Outrage." <u>United States Catholic Historical Society</u>
     <u>Records and Studies</u> 14 (1920): 7-19.

952 Trimble, Thomas J. "Bible Reading in the Public Schools."
     <u>Vanderbilt Law Review</u> 9 (June 1956): 849-60.

953 "Unconstitutionality of Statute Requiring Bible Reading
     in Public Schools." <u>Vanderbilt Law Review</u> 13 (March
     1960): 550 ff.

954 "Use of the Bible in Public Schools; Symposium."
     <u>Biblical World</u> 27 (January 1906): 48-62.

955 Vedral, Joyce. "I Teach Bible in a Public School."
     <u>Christian Herald</u> 82 (September 1982): 12.

956 Vollmar, Edward R. "The Colorado Bible Case." <u>American</u>
     <u>Ecclesiastical Review</u> 138 (March 1958): 190-95.

957 Wallace, W. J. "Bible Reading and Prayer." <u>Massachu-</u>
     <u>setts Teacher</u> 43 (November 1963): 24-25.

958 Welldon, J. E. C. "The Bible in the Schools." <u>Nine-</u>
     <u>teenth Century</u> 91 (February 1922): 317-25.

959 "What's at Stake in Florida?" <u>America</u> 103 (August 6,
     1960): 510-11.

960 Wilson, H. B. "Highschool Credits for Bible Study in
     Kansas." <u>Religious Education</u> 10 (December 1915):
     574-78.

961 Wood, Clarence Ashton. "Credit for Outside Bible Study
     in the Public Schools and Colleges of New York State."
     M.A. thesis. State University of New York (Albany),
     1916.

CHAPTER 9
TEACHING ABOUT RELIGION

Teaching objective information about religion and religious influences on secular culture is a laudable though difficult goal. Much of the material in this chapter comes from professional educators who have explored ways to integrate religious studies in the curriculum (971, 974, 986, 991, 995, 1025).

Some excellent insights can be gleaned from 965, 977, 981, 1003, 1005, 1019, and 1022-23--all authorities in this field.

Teacher evaluation and attitudes are explored in 967-970, 982, 1000, 1009.

962 Boehme, Galen Ray. "Teaching About Religion in Kansas High School Language Arts Classes, 1972-1973." Ph.D. dissertation. University of Kansas, 1974.

963 Bower, William C. "Taking Account of Religion." Kentucky School Journal 34 (April 1956): 12-13.

964 Bussert, Martha Lucille. "Attitude of a representative State Teachers College Faculty Toward the Objective Study About Religion as a Part of the Teacher Training Program." M.A. thesis. Northwestern University, 1951.

965 Coxe, Claire. The Fourth R: What Can be Taught About Religion in the Public Schools. New York: Hawthorne, 1969.

966 Cranston, Mildred W. "The Issue of Religion in Education." YWCA Magazine 57 (December 1963): 18-19.

967 Dierenfield, Richard B. "Teaching About Religion: Attitudes and Backgrounds of Beginning Teachers." Religious Education 66 (March 1971): 137-44.

968 Duffy, Eugene. "Evaluation of the Teaching of Religion in the Secondary Schools of the United States." M.A. thesis. Immaculate Heart College, 1957.

969 Durst, David. "Some Personal Reflections on Teaching High School Religion." Religious Education 63 (1968): 97-105.

970 Duvall, Sylvanus. "The Fourth R--Right-and Wrong." The National Parent Teacher 55 (December 1960): 14-16.

971 Elliott, Harrison S., and Stewart G. Cole. "Religious Education and Public Education, a Suggested Syllabus." Religious Education 35 (October-December 1940): 195-209.

972 Ferguson, J. "Teaching Religion and Teaching About Religion." Minnesota Journal of Education 48 (December 1967): 14-15.

973 Fisher, C. M. "The Place of Religious Music in the School Curriculum." Music Educators Journal 53 (November 1966): 66-67.

974 "Florida's Religion-Social Studies Curriculum Project." Educational Digest 35 (March 1970): 42-44.

975 Frankena, William K. "The Teaching of Religion: Some Guiding Principles." Religious Education 54 (March 1959): 108-09.

976 Garber, Lee Orville. "Court Sets Guidelines for Teaching About Religion." The Nation's Schools 88 (September 1971): 78.

977 Gaustad, Edwin Scott. "Teaching About Religion in the Public Schools: New Ventures in Public Education." Journal of Church and State 11 (Spring 1969): 265-76.

978 Gerard, B. S. "Teaching About Religion: When and Where to Begin." Religious Education 58 (May 1968): 215-18.

979 Goadrick, Edward W. "Religion, the Fourth 'R' in the American Public School Curriculum." M.A. thesis. Western Montana College of Education, 1956.

980 Gorr, A. "National Practices in Teaching About Religion." Educational Leadership 28 (January 1971): 411-412.

981 Henry, Virgil. "The Objective Study of Religion as a Function of Public Education." Ed.D. dissertation. Teachers College, Columbia University, 1948.

982 Hepburn, L. R. "Religion in the Social Studies: The Question of Religious Attitudes." Religious Education 66 (May 1971): 172-79.

983 Hess, M. Whitcomb. "Canon Bell: Crusador for Religious Education." Catholic World 173 (May 1951): 98-104.

984 Hirshberg, Edward W., et al. Religion in the High School Curriculum. Greenville, North Carolina: East Carolina College, 1956.

985 Hoeks, Henry Jay. "Issues and Guidelines for the Academic Study of Religion in Michigan Public Secondary Schools." Ed.D. dissertation. Columbia University Teachers College, 1976.

986 Hunt, Rolfe Lanier. "How Religion Can Fit in the Curriculum." The Nation's Schools 78 (August 1968): 38-40.

987 ————. "How Schools Can Teach Religious Values, Legally." The Nation's Schools 73 (February 1964): 48-49.

988 ————. "Teaching About Religion in the Public Schools." Today's Education 58 (December 1969): 24-26.

989 Inch, Morris Alton. "The American Heritage and Teaching About Religion." Religious Education 59 (September 1964): 400-04.

990 ————. "Teaching About Religion in the Public Schools of the United States." Th.D. dissertation. Boston University, 1955.

991 Kapaun, Emil J. "A Study of the Accrediting of Courses of Religion in the Secondary Schools of the United States." M.A. thesis. The Catholic University of America, 1948.

992 Kauffman, Albert W. "A Study of Our Public School Curricula in Relation to Religious Education." Religious Education 42 (November 1947): 326-29.

993 Kreshel, J. J. "Religion Courses for High Schools." National Catholic Educational Association, Proceedings (1936): 334-45.

994 Little, Lawrence C., ed. Religion in the Social Studies. New York: The National Conference of Christians and Jews, 1966.

995 Lucks, Henry A. "Integrating Religious Instruction and Public School Studies." Catholic Educational Review 52 (January 1954): 26-35.

996 McNall, S. G. "Make the Scientific Study of Religion Defensible." Minnesota Journal of Education 48 (December 1967): 12-13.

997 McNearney, Clayton L. "The Kanawha County Textbook Controversy." Religious Education 76 (September-October 1975): 519-40.

998 Medearis, Dale Weston. "Elements of the Curriculum of Religious Education in American Public Schools." B.D. thesis. Texas Christian University, 1946.

999 Miller, Allan Ray. "Religion in Kansas High School Social Studies." Ed.D. dissertation. University of Kansas, 1973.

1000 Miller, Harriet Lillian. "The Preparation for Teaching Religion in the Public Schools." Ph.D. dissertation. Ohio State University, 1966.

1001 Morris, Edward Alfred. "The Separation of Church and State Principle and the Use of Religious Music in the Public School." Ph.D. dissertation. University of Michigan, 1979.

1002 Nesmith, Newton Hall. "A Resource Unit About Religion that is Objective Enough for Use in American Public Schools at Levels from the Seventh through the Ninth Grades." M.S. thesis. Northern Illinois University, 1958.

1003 Nielsen, Niels C., Jr. God in Education: A New Opportunity for American Schools. New York: Sheed and Ward, 1966.

1004 Olafson, F. A. "Teaching About Religion: Some Reservations." Harvard Educational Review 37 (Spring 1967): 238-49.

1005 Panoch, James V., and David L. Barr. Religion Goes to School. New York: Harper and Row, 1968.

1006 ———. "Should We Teach About Religions in Our Public Schools?" Social Education 33 (December 1969): 910-16.

1007 Phenix, Philip H. "Why Teach Religion in the Schools?" Spectrum 47 (November 1971): 4-7.

1008 Quigley, Charles. "Reactions to Should We Teach About Religions in Our Public Schools." Social Education 33 (December 1969): 913-16.

1009 Randall, Edwin Mortimer. "What Should the Social Studies Teacher in Public Secondary Schools Teach About Religion?" M.A. thesis. Arizona State University, 1950.

1010 Raymond, S. "The Principles of Pragmatism and the Teaching of Religion in the Public School." The Catholic Educational Review 47 (June 1949): 365-79.

1011 Russell, Robert Terry. "Views of American Liberal Protestant Religious Educators 1940-1974, with Respect to Studies of Religion in Public Schools." Ph.D. dissertation. Ohio State University, 1976.

1012 "Schools Should Teach About Religions: School Administrators Opinion Poll." The Nation's Schools 67 (September 1960): 74.

1013 Shibler, Herman L. "Education About Religion." Religious Education 51 (July 1956): 270-71.

1014 ———. "You Can Teach About Religion." The Nation's Schools 60 (December 1957): 35-37.

1015 Stewart, John T. "Teaching 'About' Religion." Christian Century 72 (November 23, 1955): 1360-61.

1016 "Studying Religion in the Public Schools." Church and State 26 (December 1973): 13-14.

1017 "Teaching About Religion." The Christian Century 72 (November 23, 1955): 1360-61.

1018 "Units, Courses, and Projects for Teaching About Religions." Social Education 33 (December 1969): 917-30.

1019 Warshaw, Thayer S. Religion, Education and the Supreme Court. Nashville: Abingdon, 1979.

1020   Warshaw, Thayer S.   "Teaching About Religion in Public
         School: Eight Questions." Phi Delta Kappan 49
         (November 1967): 127-33.

1021   Will, P. J.   "Approach to Teaching About Religion in
         the Public Schools." Religious Education 66 (March
         1971): 145-48.

1022   Wood, James E., Jr.   "Religion and America's Public
         Schools." Journal of Church and State 9 (Winter
         1967): 5-16.

1023   ———.   "The Role of Religion in Public Education."
         Journal of Church and State 10 (Spring 1968): 183-89.

1024   Yeates, John W.   "Religiosity and the Public Schools."
         Church and State 28 (January 1975): 19-20.

1025   Young, William Harry.   "Teaching About Religion in
         Secondary School Social Studies." Ed.D. dissertation.
         Columbia University, 1968.

CHAPTER 10
THE BIBLE AS LITERATURE AND COMPARATIVE RELIGION

This chapter includes more specific material about such
subjects as "Bible as Literature," comparative religion, and
the use of religious music in music classes. Some pioneering
works are reviewed in 1028, 1029, 1048 and 1060. The legit-
imacy of religious music as an educational tool is explored
by 1055 and 1056. Studying Eastern religions displeases some
religious conservatives (1030 and 1036) and liberals (1047).

1026 Abbott, Lyman. "Is it Safe to Teach the Bible?" Out-
     look 129 (December 14, 1921): 596-97; 130 (January
     18, 1922): 92.

1027 Abbott, Walter M. "A Common Bible Reader for Public
     Schools." Religious Education 56 (January 1961):
     20-24.

1028 ————., and Robert F. Drinan. "A Bible Reader for
     Public Schools." America 104 (October 22, 1960):
     117-19.

1029 Ackerman, James S. "The Indiana University Summer
     Institute on Teaching the Bible in Secondary English."
     Journal of Church and State 14 (Autumn 1972): 457-74.

1030 Adeney, Frances. "Some Schools Are Looking East for
     Answers." Moody Monthly 82 (May 1982): 18-20.

1031 Adler, Morris. "Religion and Public Schools--The
     Greater Opportunity." Religious Education 44 (March
     1949): 72-75.

1032 Aldrich, Emerson L. "A Survey of Religious Education
     in the Public High Schools in Indiana." M.S. thesis.
     Indiana State University (Terre Haute), 1948.

1033 Allen, Charles Frederick. "Bible Teaching in the Pub-
     lic Schools." Th.M. thesis. Union Theological Sem-
     inary (Richmond), 1950.

1034   Allen, Jack. "The Study of Religion in High School
       American History." Religious Education 52 (July
       1957): 282-87.

1035   Anderson, Henrietta. "Some Aspects of Religious Educa-
       tion and the Public Schools." M.S. thesis. Univer-
       sity of North Dakota, 1952.

1036   Baltazar, E. R. "T M and the Religion-in-School Issue."
       Christian Century 93 (August 18, 1976): 708-09.

1037   Bartel, R. "Teaching the Bible as Literature." Oregon
       Education 41 (December 1966): 6-7.

1038   Boddy, William H., and Helen L. Clair. "The Biblical
       Knowledge of High School Students." Religious Educa-
       tion 9 (August 1914): 375-81.

1039   Boone, R. G. "Secular Uses of the Bible." Education
       22 (November 1901): 129-40.

1040   Boutwell, W. D. "No Ban on Bible Study." PTA Magazine
       63 (February 1969): 14.

1041   Boyle, Robert Driscoll. "The Use of the Bible in the
       Public Schools." M.A. thesis. Southern Methodist
       University, 1940.

1042   Bracler, J. F. "Toward a Discovery of Western Reli-
       gions." Independent School Bulletin 31 (December
       1971): 59-60.

1043   Briles, Charles W. "The Oklahoma Plan of Bible Study
       Credits." Religious Education 11 (June 1916): 285-87.

1044   Brown, E. H. "Life of Christ in the Upper Sandusky
       High School." School Review 31 (November 1923):
       704-06.

1045   Crawl, Ray. "A Course of Study for Teaching of Bible
       in the High School." M.A. thesis. Indiana State
       University (Terre Haute), 1932.

1046   "Curriculum and Our Religious Heritage." Theory Into
       Practice 4 (February 1965): 29-32.

1047   Doerr, Edd. "Transcendental Meditation Goes to School."
       Church and State 27 (October 1974): 1, 6.

1048 Forcinelli, Joseph. "The History of World Religions:
     A Course as Taught at the Claremont, California,
     High School." Journal of Secondary Education 42
     (April 1967): 162-165.

1049 Hamilton, J. T. "Teaching Comparative Religion in
     Public Schools." Education 87 (November 1966): 177-
     179.

1050 Hansen, Wendell Jay. "An Iowa Experiment in Public
     School Bible Teaching." Ph.D. thesis. University of
     Iowa, 1947.

1051 Hogan, R.F. "The Bible in the English Program." Eng-
     lish Journal 54 (September 1965): 488-494.

1052 Lehman, Daniel Webster. "What the Bible Contributes
     to Secondary Education." M.A. thesis. University of
     Virginia, 1925.

1053 Marratt, H. "Comparative Study of Religion in Schools."
     Religious Education 64 (January 1969): 30-36.

1054 Russell, W.H. "The New Testament as a Text in High
     School Religion." The Catholic Educational Review
     27 (September 1929): 385-401.

1055 Seamman, J. "Religious Music in the Public Schools."
     Music Educators Journal 58 (May 1967): 46-49.

1056 Schwadron, A. "On Religion, Music, and Education."
     Journal of Research in Music Education 18 (Summer
     1970): 157-166.

1057 Smart, N. "Comparative Study of Religions and the
     Schools." Religious Education 64 (January 1969):
     26-30.

1058 Vanderzee, Andrew. "Religious Education Through Social
     Studies and Literature in Secondary Schools." M.A.
     thesis. Western Michigan University, 1942.

1059 Warshaw, Thayer S. Bible Related Curriculum Materials.
     Nashville: Abingdon, 1976.

1060 Whitney, John R. "Introducing Religious Literature in
     Pennsylvania Secondary Schools." Religious Education
     63 (1968): 89-96.

CHAPTER 11
RELEASED TIME

Releasing students for a designated period of time for off-
campus religious instruction has experienced periods of popularity during this century. The "released time" concept
gained strength around the First World War and retained its
relative popularity until the late 1940s. However, certain
zealous religious groups convinced school authorities that it
was easier and more efficient to move the instruction classes
on to school property. This resulted in the famous McCollum
decision of the U. S. Supreme Court in 1948, striking down
this arrangement as unconstitutional. Four years later the
High Court clarified its position in the Zorach decision and
held that released time off campus property was constitutionally permissible.

This chapter looks at how released time has worked in various states and communities and how the various religious tradi-
tions have attempted to meet the challenges and opportunities
posed by the concept.

Many of the citations address the Court's McCollum ruling,
often critically, as in 1159 and 1168. Citations 1167 and
1183 look at the impact of the decision on local school districts.

    1061 Alfred, Vincent C. Legal Aspects of Released Time.
          Washington, D.C.: National Catholic Welfare
          Conference, 1946.

    1062 Antieau, C. J. "Limitation of Religious Liberty."
          Fordham Law Review 18 (November 1949): 221-41.

    1063 Archdeacon, John Philip. "The Weekday Religious
          School." Ph.D. dissertation. Catholic University
          of America, 1927.

    1064 Bacon, Fred Mason. "Contributions of Catholic
          Religious Orders to Public Education in New Mexico
          since the American Occupation." M.A. thesis.
          University of New Mexico, 1947.

1065 Beckes, Isaac K. "Interfaith Attitudes in Weekday
      Religious Education." Ph.D. dissertation. Yale
      University, 1946.

1066 Bennett, John C. "Implication of the New Conception
      of 'Separation.'" Christianity and Crisis 8:89-90.

1067 Berner, Sister M. Ethelberge, O.S.F. "A Study of
      Plans and Opportunities for Religious Instruction
      on Released Time Basis." M.A. thesis. De Paul
      University, 1948.

1068 Bodden, Rosalind V. "Released Time." M.A. thesis.
      State Teachers College (Newark, N.J.), 1954.

1069 Borowski, Maria C.R. "Released Time for Religious
      Instruction: A Reappraisal." Education 68
      (December 1947): 205-07.

1070 Bower, William Clayton. "Religion on Released Time."
      Christian Century 58 (August 6, 1941): 980-81.

1071 Boyer, W. W., Jr. "Religious Education of Public
      School Pupils in Wisconsin: Sectarian Instruction
      of Public School Pupils; Release of Public School
      Pupils for Religious Instruction." Wisconsin Law
      Review (March 1953): 181-255.

1072 Broden, Thomas F. "Church and State--Excusing of
      Public School Pupils for Religious Instruction."
      Notre Dame Lawyer 22 (March 1947): 360-62.

1073 Bruce, Homer L., Jr. "Constitutional Law--Released-
      Time Religious Education--Laws Respecting an Estab-
      lishment of Religion." Texas Law Review 27
      (December 1948): 256-59.

1074 Carpenter, William Weston. "Education Without
      Religion." Phi Delta Kappan 29 (May 1948): 368-70.

1075 Cavert, Walter D. "Ban Religion in Public Schools."
      Christian Century 62 (July 25, 1945): 868-69.

1076 ————. "Six Values in 'Released Time.'" Christian
      Century 74 (December 4, 1957): 1445-46.

1077 "The Champaign Case." Christian Century 65 (April 7,
      1948): 308-09.

1078 Clyde, Walter R. "Religion in Puertò Rican Politics."
      Christian Century 61 (October 11, 1944): 1167-69.

1079 Collins, Joseph B. "Released Time for Catholic
      Children." Religious Education 41 (January 1946):
      20-21.

1080 ————. "Released Time for Religious Education."
      American Ecclesiastical Review 115 (July 1946):
      11-23 and (August 1946): 121-37.

1081 Corbett, William D. "The Status of Public Knowledge
      Concerning the Program of Released Time for Reli-
      gious Education: A Case Study." M.A. thesis.
      Boston College, 1954.

1082 Corcoran, Gertrude B. "Release-Time Religious
      Education in the Elementary School." M.Ed. thesis.
      San Jose State College, 1953.

1083 Corwin, Edward S. "The Supreme Court as National
      School Board." Thought 43 (December 1948): 665-83.

1084 Cummings, J. Joseph. "Constitutional Law, Church
      and State: Validity of the 'Released Time' Program."
      Marquette Law Review 35 (Spring 1952): 385-90.

1085 Cutton, George Leon. "Released Time—No Violation of
      the American Principle." International Journal
      of Religious Education 19 (September 1942): 12-13.

1086 Davis, Mary Dabney. "Release of Public-School Pupils
      for Weekday Classes in Religious Education."
      School Life 26 (July 1941): 299-301.

1087 ————. Week-Day Religious Instruction. Washington,
      D.C.: U. S. Government Printing Office, 1933.

1088 ————. Week-Day Classes in Religious Education.
      Washington, D.C.: U. S. Government Printing Office,
      1941.

1089 ————. "Weekday Classes in Religious Education
      Conducted on Released School Time for Public-School
      Pupils." U. S. Office of Education Bulletin 3
      (1941): 1-66. "Summary." School Life 26 (July
      1941): 299-301.

1090   "Dismissal of Pupils for Religious Instruction Held
       to Be Legal." School Review 34 (June 1926): 400-03.

1091   Drinan, Robert F., S.J. "The Lawyers and Religion."
       America 80 (March 5, 1949): 593-95.

1092   ————. "McCollum Decision: Three Years After."
       America 84 (February 24, 1951): 611-13.

1093   ————. "Novel 'Liberty' Created by the McCollum
       Decision." Georgetown Law Journal 39 (January
       1951): 216-41.

1094   ————. "The Supreme Court and Religion." Commonweal
       41 (September 12, 1952): 554-56.

1095   Dushkin, A. M. "Legality of Released Time in New
       York." Jewish Education 19 (Summer 1948): 8-10.

1096   ————. "Religion and the Public Schools." Jewish
       Education 17 (June 1946): 3-4.

1097   Eby, Kermit. "What Can a Teacher Believe?" Progressive
       Education 3 (March 1937): 158-62.

1098   Edidin, Ben M. "Released Time in the Jewish Community."
       Religious Education 41 (January 1946): 16-19.

1099   Edmondson, J. B. "Teachers' Opinions on Religion and
       the Public Schools." Religious Education 42 (Nov-
       ember 1947): 330-32.

1100   Elbin, Paul N. "Religion in State Schools." Christian
       Century 69 (September 17, 1952): 1061-63.

1101   Fey, Harold E. "Test Legality of Released Time."
       Christian Century 62 (September 26, 1945): 1099-1100.

1102   Fine, Benjamin. "Religion and the Public Schools."
       Menorah Journal 32 (April 1944): 93-101.

1103   Fingerit, Irwin K. "The Released Time Program for
       Religious Instruction and the Courts." M.A. thesis.
       New York University, 1956.

1104   Fox, George G. "An Old Issue in a New Guise."
       Christian Century 58 (August 20, 1941): 1027-30.

1105 Franer, William A. "Religious Instruction on Released School Time." M.A. thesis. Catholic University of America, 1942.

1106 Franklin, John L. "Education and Religion." Phi Delta Kappan 29 (May 1948): 365-68.

1107 Frasher, Velma. "The Interfaith Committee and the Released-Time Program." International Journal of Religious Education 38 (July 1962): 16-17.

1108 Fulcher, Beatrice Card. "Weekday Religious Education on Released Time in New York City." Education 71 (February 1951): 385-88.

1109 Garber, Lee O. "Zorach Case." The Nation's Schools 50 (August 1952): 67-68.

1110 Gauss, Christian. "Should Religion Be Taught in Our Schools?" Ladies' Home Journal 65 (September 1948): 40+.

1111 Gerig, Jared Franklin. "The Legal Status of Religious Education on Released Time." M.A. thesis. Arizona State University, 1945.

1112 Gillis, Frederick J. "Weekly Religious Education-- Boston Public Schools." Education 71 (February 1951): 375-81.

1113 Gorham, Donald Rex. A Study of the Status of Weekday Church Schools in the United States. Philadelphia: School of Religious Education, Eastern Baptist Theological Seminary, 1934.

1114 Gosnell, John W. "Released Time Religious Education in Virginia." M.A. thesis. De Paul University, 1935.

1115 Greenbaum, Edward S. and Thayer, Vivian Trow. "Released Time: The Parents' Right to Choose.--Released Time, a Crutch for the Churches." The Nation 174 (February 9, 1952): 128-32.

1116 Hansen, Roland H. "The Status of the Released-Time Program in Weekday Religious Education from the McCollum Case to the Present." B.D. thesis. Wartburg Theological Seminary, 1954.

1117 Harris, Elizabeth. "Protestant Weekday Religious
      Education in Boston." Education 71 (February
      1951): 382-84.

1118 Hartnett, Robert C. "Alternatives to Released Time."
      America 80 (October 16, 1948): 37-39.

1119 ———. "The McCollum Case." America (April 24,
      1948): 49-52.

1120 ———. "Aftermath of the McCollum Decision." America
      79 (September 25, 1948): 561-63.

1121 ———. "Is the 'Wall of Separation' an Iron Curtain?"
      America 83 (April 22, 1950): 75.

1122 ———. "Religious Education and the Constitution."
      America 87 (May 17, 1952): 195-97 and (May 24,
      1952): 223-26.

1123 Hess, Mrs. M. Whitcomb. "A Devil Newly Invented!
      Released Time Case; Reply to A.E. Meyer." The
      Catholic World 168 (January 1949): 295-301.

1124 Hill, Horatio Seymour. "A Case for the Released Time
      School." Religious Education 40 (May-June 1945):
      172-73.

1125 Hodgdon, Daniel R. "Excusing Public-School Pupils
      for Religious Instruction." The Clearing House 23
      (February 1949): 374-75.

1126 ———. "Religious Instruction in a School Building."
      The Clearing House 23 (March 1949): 436-37.

1127 Howlett, Walter M. "The Case for Released Time."
      Education 71 (February 1951): 370-74.

1128 ———. "Released Time for Religious Education in
      New York City." Education 64 (May 1944): 523-25.

1129 ———. "Released Time for Religious Education in
      New York City." Religious Education 37 (March
      April 1942): 104-08.

1130 Hurd, Arthur Bentley. "Status of the Curriculum of
      the Protestant Released Time Weekday Church School
      in Ohio." M.Ed. thesis. Kent State University,
      1950.

1131 Hurwich, Louis. "Religious Education and the Release-Time Plan." Jewish Education 13 (September 1941): 103-07.

1132 Hynson, Leon Orville. "The Church and Public School in Cooperation, A Study of Released Time." M.A. thesis. University of Delaware, 1963.

1133 Johnson, F. Ernest. "An Issue that Needs Rethinking." Christianity and Crisis 12 (August 1952): 105-06.

1134 Jorgensen, Leroy I. "Weekday Religious Education on Released Time and the History of South Cache Seminary." M.A. thesis. Utah State Agricultural College, 1957.

1135 Keesecker, W. W. Laws Relating to the Releasing of Pupils from Public Schools for Religious Instruction. Washington, D.C.: Superintendent of Documents, 1933.

1136 Knight, Edgar W. "Released School Time and Religious Education, 1948." School Management 17 (July 1948): 3+.

1137 Larson, Jordan L. and Tapp, Robert B. "Released Time for Religious Education?--Yes, says Jordan L. Larson; No, says Robert B. Tapp." National Education Association Journal 47 (November 1958): 572-74.

1138 Lassiter, James M. "The McCollum Decision and the Public School." Kentucky Law Journal 37 (May 1949): 402-11.

1139 Logan, S. R. "Religious Resources of the Teacher." School and Society 15 (May 27, 1922): 591-92.

1140 MacGrath, (Sister) Mary. "Brady Plan in a Detroit School." America 74 (February 9, 1946): 510-11.

1141 Manion, Clarence. The Church, the State, and Mrs. McCollum. Notre Dame, Indiana: Ave Maria Press, 1950.

1142 Martin, John Patrick. "History of the Released Time Religious Education in the Schools of Chelsea from 1941 to 1946." M.Ed. thesis. Boston College, 1946.

1143   McClure, Lois V. "Weekday Religious Education at the
       High School Level." M.A. thesis. Northwestern
       University, 1951.

1144   McCollum, Vashti. One Woman's Fight. New York:
       Doubleday, 1951.

1145   McNamee, Brother Marion. "Released Time Program in
       the Archdiocese and the Dioceses of New York."
       M.A. thesis. Boston College, 1950.

1146   McNeill, L.A. "Diocesan Superintendent and the
       Religious Instruction of Public-School Pupils."
       National Catholic Education Association Proceedings
       (1932): 488-96.

1147   McPherson, Imogene M., et al. "Released Time in
       New York City, A Symposium." Religious Education
       38 (January-February 1943): 15-24.

1148   Meyer, Agnes E. "The Clerical Challenge to the
       Schools." The Atlantic Monthly 189 (March 1952):
       42-46. Discussion 189 (May 1952): 22-23 and
       (June 1952): 21-23.

1149   ————. "The School, the State, and the Church."
       The Atlantic Monthly 182 (November 1948): 45-50.

1150   Moehlman, Arthur B. "Released Time." The Nation's
       Schools 40 (November 1947): 18-19.

1151   Moehlman, Conrad Henry. "The Wall of Separation:
       the Law and the Facts." American Bar Association
       Journal 38 (April 1952): 281-84, 343-48.

1152   Mones, Leon. "Religious Education and the Public
       Schools." The Clearing House 15 (March 1941):
       395-96.

1153   Morrisson, Charles Clayton. "What Did the Supreme
       Court Say?" Christian Century 66 (June 8, 1949):
       707-09.

1154   Mulford, Herbert B. "The Illinois 'Atheist' Case."
       School and Society 65 (June 21, 1947): 461-62.

1155 ————. "The Supreme Court Sets Hurdles in Religion
        for the American School Board." American School
        Board Journal 116 (April 1948): 37-39.

1156 National Education Association of the United States,
        Research Division. "The Released-Time Decision."
        National Education Association Journal 37 (April
        1948): 209-10.

1157 "New York City Provision for Released Time for Reli-
        gious Education." The Elementary School Journal
        41 (February 1941): 411.

1158 "The New York City Public School 'Release Time Plan'
        for Religious Instruction--A Symposium." Jewish
        Education 12 (January 1941): 157-65.

1159 O'Byrne, John P. "God and Our Government." St. John's
        Law Review 23 (April 1949): 292-96.

1160 O'Gara, Sister Mary Joan. "The Teaching of Religion
        in the Tax-Supported Schools of Illinois: The
        McCollum Decision and Its Historical Background."
        M.A. thesis. De Paul University, 1950.

1161 O'Neill, James M. "The Supreme Court on the Separation
        of Church and State." Commonweal 49 (February 18,
        1949): 466-69.

1162 ————, and Cohler, M. J. Supreme Court Decision on
        Religious Education. Evanston: Northwestern
        University, 1948.

1163 "One-Woman Crusade Against Religion." America 80
        (November 27, 1948): 198-99.

1164 Owen, Ralph Dornfield. "The McCollum Case." Temple
        Law Quarterly 22 (October 1948): 159-73.

1165 Parsons, Wilfrid, S.J. "No Religion in the Schools/"
        Sign 27 (May 1948): 12-14.

1166 Patrick, Gordon. "The Impact of a Court Decision:
        Aftermath of the McCollum Case." Journal of Public
        Law 6 (Fall 1957): 455-64.

1167 ————. "The Impact of the McCollum Decision Particularly in Illinois." Ph.D. dissertation. University of Illinois, 1957.

1168 Powers, Francis Joseph. "The Supreme Court and the Constitutional Prohibition Against 'an establishment of religion.'" The Jurist 12 (July 1952): 282-314.

1169 "Progress in Weekday Religious Education—A Symposium." Religious Education 41 (January-February 1946): 6-25.

1170 "Protestants: Come Clean!" Christian Century 65 (June 16, 1948): 591-92.

1171 Reed, George E. "Church-State and the Zorach Case." Notre Dame Lawyer 27 (Summer 1952): 529-551.

1172 "Released Time Considered: The New York Plan is Tested." Yale Law Journal 62 (March 1952): 405-16.

1173 "Released Time Lawful in New York State." Christian Century 65 (December 1, 1948): 1292-93.

1174 "Released Time in New York City—A Symposium." Religious Education 38 (January 1943): 15-24.

1175 "Released Time in Chicago: A Panel Discussion on Superintendent William H. Johnson's Proposal to Offer Released Time and Credit for Religious Education in Churches in Chicago." Religious Education 36 (April 1941): 112-16.

1176 "Releasing the Time." Commonweal 47 (March 26, 1948): 581-82.

1177 "Religious Education and the Public Schools." High School Journal 31 (May 1948): 99-111.

1178 "Religious Instruction in the Public School System." Columbia Law Review 47 (December 1947): 1346-55.

1179 Remmlein, Madaline Kinter. "The Legal Situation Resulting from the Recent Supreme Court Decision." Religious Education 43 (July-August 1948): 211-16.

1180 "Salvaging Released Time." <u>Christian Century</u> 65 (May· 5, 1948): 405-06.

1181 Schug, Philip Charles. "The .Winnetka School· System Contributes to Religious Education." B.D. thesis. Chicago Theological Seminary, 1942.

1182 Shaver, Erwin L. "Significant Aspects of the River Forest Plan." <u>Religious Education</u> 35 (October-December 1940): 231-35.

1183 ————. "Three Years After the Champaign Case." <u>Religious Education</u> 46 (January 1951): 33-38.

1184 ————. "Weekday Religious Education, a Significant Addition to the Churches' Teaching Program." <u>Education</u> 71 (February 1951): 365-69.

1185 ————. "Weekday Religious Education Secures Its Charter and Faces a Challenge." <u>Religious Education</u> 48 (January-February 1953): 38-43.

1186 Slavin, Robert. "Released Time for Religious Education in Illinois." M.S. thesis. Northern Illinois University, 1964.

1187 Sloan, Paul W. "Released Time for Sectarian Religious Instruction." <u>Educational Administration and Supervision</u> 33 (March 1947): 154-56.

1188 Smith, Thomas L., Jr. "Separation of Church and State in Public Schools." <u>Alabama Law Review</u> 7 (Fall 1954): 99-107.

1189 Sorauf, Frank J. "Zorach v. Clauson: The Impact of a Supreme Court Decision." <u>American Political Science Review</u> 53 (September 1959): 777-79.

1190 Stolworthy, Reed L. "A Study of the Legal Provisions Relating to Released Time for Religious Study and to Religion in Public Education." M.S. thesis. Brigham Young University, 1959.

1191 Storm, H. C. "The Batavia Plan of Week-Day Religious Instruction." <u>The Elementary School Journal</u> 21 (April 1921): 625-29.

1192   "Supreme Court Bans Released Time." Christian Century
       65 (March 17, 1948): 294.

1193   Sutherland, Arthur E., Jr. "Due Process and Dises-
       tablishment." Harvard Law Review 62 (June 1949):
       1306-44.

1194   Swancara, Frank. The Separation of Religion and
       Government: The First Amendment, Madison's Intent,
       and the McCollum Decision; A Study of Separationism
       in America. New York: Truth Seeker Co., 1950.

1195   Taylor, T. Raber. "Equal Protection of Religion:
       Today's Public School Problem." American Bar
       Association Journal 38 (April 1952):   335-42.

1196   Thompson, Kenneth L. Weekday Religious Education
       in the High Schools of the United States. Phila-
       delphia: Eastern Baptist Theological Seminary,
       1938.

1197   "'Time-Off' in the Public Schools for Religious
       Instruction." School and Society 53 (May 10, 1941):
       596-97.

1198   Tuttle, Albert Theodore. "Released Time Religious
       Education Program of the Church of Jesus Christ
       of Latter-Day Saints." M.A. thesis. Stanford
       University, 1949.

1199   Van Vleet, W.B., Jr. "Constitutional Law--Result
       of the 'Everson Amendment'--The McCollum Case."
       Marquette Law Review 32 (September 1948):   138-45.

1200   Wagener, Anthony P. "A Factual and Legal History of
       the Use of Released Time for Religious Instruction
       for Pupils Attending Public Schools." M.A. thesis.
       Catholic University of America, 1947.

1201   Walker, Harvey, Sr. "Church and State, 1948." Ohio
       State Law Journal 9 (Spring 1948):   336-42.

1202   Walters, Raymond. "Religion in Our Lives as
       Educators." National Association of Secondary
       School Principals Bulletin 36 (April 1952): 379-84.

1203 Waterhouse, Howard A. "Is Released Time Worth While?"
      Christian Century 74 (October 2, 1957): 1164-66.

1204 "Weekday Religious Education in Your Future." Inter-
      national Journal of Religious Education 36 (June
      1960): 5-11.

1205 Wetzel, William A. "Religious Education--A Layman's
      Analysis." National Association of Secondary-
      School Principals, Bulletin 33 (October 1949):
      66-74.

1206 Whiteside, Robert J. "The Released Time Program of
      the Diocese of Buffalo." M.A. thesis. Boston
      College, 1952.

1207 Wilkins, Ruth W. "Constitutionality of the Utah Re-
      leased Time Program." Utah Law Review 3 (Spring
      1953): 329-39.

1208 Willett, Sallie Siler. "The McCollum Case and Reli-
      gious Instruction in Tennessee Public Schools."
      M.S. thesis. University of Tennessee, 1950.

1209 Winters, Marguerite. "The Weekday Church School
      in California." Religious Education 40 (January-
      February 1945): 43-71.

1210 Wirt, William M. "The Gary Public Schools and the
      Churches." Religious Education 11 (June 1916):
      221-26.

1211 Yerden, Elsie M. "Released Time for Religion in
      Public Schools." M.A. thesis. Western Michigan
      College (Kalamazoo), 1955.

1212 Zion, Joel. "Developments in Released Time." Jewish
      Education 19 (Fall 1947): 39-44.

CHAPTER 12
RELIGIOUS INSTRUCTION AND WEEKDAY RELIGIOUS EDUCATION

Closely related to released time is the "weekday religious education" movement in the early days of the twentieth century. This church-school partnership was promoted as an ideal solution by many religious leaders and educators. But its impact was greatest in religiously homogeneous areas where religious minorities were unable or unwilling to protest.

Religious "instruction," as opposed to objective study "of" religion, was promoted by this movement, and was popular with many Catholics and evangelical Protestants. It was less than popular among those who believed that religious instruction is a function properly reserved to families and churches.

1213 Allan, E.M. "Survey of Week Day Schools in the Churches of Brooklyn Under the Supervision of the Department of Religious Education of the Brooklyn Federation of Churches." M.R.E. thesis. Biblical Seminary in New York, 1931.

1214 Asbury, Jean. "A Historical Study of Week Day Church Schools on Released Time in Gary, Indiana, from 1914 to 1948." M.R.E. thesis. Asbury Theological Seminary, 1949.

1215 Barnes, William Henry. "Current Practices and Trends in Week-Day Religious Education in Public Schools in the State of Virginia." M.A. thesis. Boston University, 1939.

1216 Bartlett, Edward R. "Measurable Moral and Religious Outcomes of Week-Day Religious Instruction." Religious Education 29 (January 1934): 25-34.

1217 ———. "Measurable Moral and Religious Outcomes of Week-Day Religious Instruction." Ph.D. dissertation. Northwestern University, 1933.

1218   Blair, W.D. "The Case for the Weekday Church School."
       Frontiers of Democracy 7 (December 1940): 75-77.

1219   Bolmeier, Edward Claude. "Legality and Propriety of
       Religious Instruction in the Public Schools."
       Educational Forum 20 (March 1956): 473-82.

1220   Brubacher, John S. "The Public School and Religious
       Instruction." *School and Society* 24 (November 20,
       1926): 621-25.

1221   Campbell, Sister Margaret. "Religious Instruction
       and Public Education." M.A. thesis. De Paul
       University, 1953.

1222   Chaffee, Charles E. "Why Weekday Religious Educa-
       cation?" *International Journal of Religious Educa-
       tion* 37 (December 1960): 22-23.

1223   Cloyd, D.E. "Weekday Religious Instruction." *Review
       of Reviews* 69 (February 1924): 188-92.

1224   Comey, Lillian Elaine. "The History and Contribution
       of the 'Virginia Weekday Religious Education Move-
       ment.'" M.A. thesis. Boston University, 1947.

1225   Connell, Francis J., C.S.S.R. "Religious Instruction
       in the Public Schools." *American Ecclesiastical
       Review* 135 (September 1956): 199-201.

1226   "Constitutional Law--Voluntary Religious Instruction
       in Public Schools--Violation of the First and
       Fourteenth Amendments." *George Washington Law
       Review* 16 (June 1948): 56-61.

1227   "Court Ruling on the White Plains Religious Instruc-
       tion Case." *School and Society* 23 (May 1, 1926):
       550-51.

1228   Courter, Claude V. "256,000 Children are Enrolled
       in Weekday Religious Schools." *The Nation's
       Schools* 9 (June 1932): 30.

1229   ————. "Administration of Schools of Weekday Reli-
       gious Education in Cities of More Than 100,000,
       abstract." National Education Association, Depart-
       ment of Superintendence, *Official Report* (1931):
       232-33.

1230 Curry, G. M. "The Present Status of the Proposal for
      Religious Instruction in the Public Schools as Seen
      by Representative Christian Leaders." B.D. thesis.
      Emory University, 1941.

1231 Cutton, George Leon. "A Critical Study of Weekday
      Religious Education in the United States." Ph.D.
      dissertation. Cornell University, 1933.

1232 ———. "History of Weekday Religious Education."
      International Journal of Religious Education 10
      (February 1934): 18-19.

1233 Elliott, Harrison S. "Are Weekday Church Schools
      the Solution?" International Journal of Religious
      Education 17 (November 1940): 8-9+.

1234 Engle, Thelburn LaRoy. "Some Phases of Weekday
      Religious Education with Special Reference to
      Correlation with the Public School." M.A. thesis.
      Northwestern University, 1924.

1235 Ernst, Rose Mary. "Weekday Religious Education for
      Catholic Pupils in the St. Louis Public Schools,
      1939-1942." M.A. thesis. St. Louis University,
      1945.

1236 "Fifty Years of Weekday Religious Education: A
      Feature Section." International Journal of Religious
      Education 40 (June 1964): 4-13.

1237 Fister, James Blaine. "Weekday Religious Education
      and Its Status in Pennsylvania." B.D. thesis.
      Lancaster Theological Seminary, 1945.

1238 Forsyth, Nathaniel Frederick. "A Survey of the Week
      Day Religious Education System of Hammond, Indiana."
      Ph.D. dissertation. Northwestern University, 1927.

1239 Gates, Goodrich. "What People Are Asking About Week-
      day Religious Education." International Journal
      of Religious Education 18 (February 1942): 12-13.

1240 Goddard, Alice L. "A New Trend in Weekday Religious
      Education." Religious Education 55 (July 1960):
      288-92.

1241 ———. "Weekday Church School--A Bridge." Inter-
      national Journal of Religious Education 34 (May
      1958): 12-13.

1242 ———. "Weekday Religious Education in Detroit."
      Religious Education 37 (September 1942): 294-98.

1243 Goldman, L. "Implications of Religious Instruction
      in Public Schools." Education 59 (January 1939):
      269-73.

1244 Goodwin, Edward J. "The Exclusion of Religious
      Instruction from the Public Schools." Educational
      Review 35 (February 1908): 129-38.

1245 Gove, Floyd S. Religious Education on Public School
      Time. Cambridge: Harvard University, 1926.

1246 Gwynn, P. H., Jr. "Week-Day Religious Education in
      North Carolina." Religious Education 39 (May-
      June 1944): 169-74.

1247 Hall, Charles A. "A Study of Week-Day Religious
      Education in Kansas." M.A. thesis. University
      of Kansas, 1926.

1248 Hanus, P. H. "School Instruction in Religion."
      Education 27 (September 1906): 10-17, 73-84.

1249 Hawkins, Mabel. 'A Study of Weekday Religious In-
      struction in Saint Louis, Missouri." M.A. thesis.
      Washington University (St. Louis), 1941.

1250 Humble, A. H. "On Religious Instruction in the
      School." Scholastic 36 (June 1948): 612-15.

1251 Israel, Edward L. "Weekday Religious Education in
      Connection with the Public School." Jewish
      Education 13 (September 1941): 99-102.

1252 Jones, Eleanor W. "The Batavia Plan for Weekday
      Religious Education." M.S. thesis. Northern
      Illinois University, 1962.

1253 Kandel, I. L. "The Public Schools and Religious
      Instruction." School and Society 73 (June 23, 1951):
      395-96.

1254 Kelley, R. B. "Weekday Religious Education in Lock-
      port, New York." New York State Education 18
      (February 1931): 575-76.

1255 Kelsey, Alice G. "Weekday Religious Education Suc-
      ceeds." International Journal of Religious Educa-
      tion 15 (January 1939): 19+.

1256 Koehler, Robert Louis, Jr. "A Study of the Program
      of Weekday Religious Education for Senior High
      School Students of Harrisburg, Pennsylvania."
      S.T.M. thesis. Lutheran Theological Seminary
      (Philadelphia), 1944.

1257 Koos, Leonard V. "Weekday Religious Instruction."
      The School Review 50 (January 1942): 8-9.

1258 Lee, Helen Marker. "A Critical Study of Weekday
      Religious Education in the State of Ohio." M.A.
      thesis. Oberlin College, 1949.

1259 LeValley, R. "Weekday Religious Education in the
      Public Schools in North Carolina." High School
      Journal 30 (March 1947): 77-84.

1260 Lewis, Hazel A. "A Case for the Weekday Church
      School." International Journal of Religious Edu-
      cation 17 (November 1940): 10-11+.

1261 Lindecker, Wayne M., Jr. "Can 'Weekday' Do the Job?"
      International Journal of Religious Education 40
      (June 1964): 10-11.

1262 Lotz, Philip Henry. "A Survey of Week-Day Religious
      Education." Ph.D. dissertation. Northwestern
      University, 1924.

1263 Magnes, J. L. "Attitude of the Jews Toward Week-Day
      Religious Instruction." Religious Education 11
      (June 1916): 226-30.

1264 McClure, Lois V. "They Want Weekday Religious Edu-
      cation; A Survey of Reactions to the Champaign Case
      Decision." International Journal of Religious Edu-
      cation 25 (September 1948): 7-8.

1265 ———. "Weekday Religious Education at the High
      School Level." Religious Education 56 (November
      1951): 345-63.

1266 McDevitt, Philip R. "The Problem of Curriculum for
      Week-Day Religious Instruction from the Roman
      Catholic Viewpoint." Religious Education 11 (June
      1916): 231-38.

1267 McGibony, John W. "The Administration of Week-Day
      Religious Education for Public School Children."
      M.Ed. thesis. University of Oklahoma, 1931.

1268 McKendry, James B. "Correlation of Week-Day Religious
      Education with the Public School Program." Reli-
      gious Education 42 (July 1947): 202-07.

1269 McKibben, Frank M. "Principles and Points in the
      Correlation of Week-Day Religious Education and
      Public Education." M.A. thesis. Northwestern
      University, 1924.

1270 ———. "Trends in Weekday Religious Education."
      Education 64 (May 1944): 525-27.

1271 ———. "Weekday Religious Instruction in Evanston."
      Missionary Review of the World 45 (November 1922):
      889-90.

1272 McKown, E. M. "A Unified Approach to Weekday Religious
      Education." International Journal of Religious
      Education 29 (May 1953): 18-19.

1273 McWhirter, Mary E. "After Thirty Years." Religious
      Education 42 (September 1947): 301-05.

1274 Merritt, J. H. "Religious Instruction in the School."
      Scholastic 30 (February 1942): 493-95.

1275 Meyer, Henry H. "The Curriculum of Week-Day Religious
      Instruction Considered from the Protestant View-
      point." Religious Education 11 (June 1916): 239-44.

1276 Miller, Minor C. "Rural Weekday Schools in Virginia."
      International Journal of Religious Education 7
      (June 1931): 22-23.

1277 "New York Again Wins Victory for Weekday Religious
      Education." International Journal of Religious
      Education 27 (September 1950): 36.

1278 Osteyee, Edith T. "A Successful Weekday Program."
      International Journal of Religious Education 24
      (November 1947): 6-7.

1279 Poe, Hillary Wood. "A Study of Weekday Religious
      Education in Hamilton County." M.Ed. thesis.
      University of Cincinnati, 1938.

1280 Priestley, Faith Orrie. "A Critique and Evaluation
      of the Week-Day Church School Movement." M.A.
      thesis. Oberlin College, 1937.

1281 Regan, Richard J. "Dilemma of Religious Instruction
      and the Public Schools." Catholic Lawyer 10
      (Winter 1964): 42+.

1282 "Religious Instruction for Public School Children."
      The Catholic World 152 (March 1941): 745-46.

1283 "Religious Instruction in Public Institutions."
      Educational Review 66 (October 1923): 170-72.

1284 "Religious Instruction in Public Schools." The
      Catholic World 118 (October 1923): 112-13.

1285 Rest, Friederich. "Weekday Schools Recruit for Sun-
      day Schools." International Journal of Religious
      Education 24 (September 1947): 14-15.

1286 Rogers, Verne Carl. "A Study of Types of Religious
      Instruction for American Public School Children."
      M.S. thesis. Purdue University, 1925.

1287 Ronning, Harold Gerhard. "Weekday Religious Education
      in Minneapolis." M.A. thesis. University of
      Minnesota, 1913.

1288 Rosenberger, Mabel. "The Growth of Weekday Church
      Schools in Wichita, Kansas, 1924-1949." M.A. thesis.
      University of Wichita, 1949.

1289 Royal, Frank E. "A Southern Baptist Program of Week-
      day Religious Education." D.R.E. dissertation.
      Southwestern Baptist Theological Seminary (Texas),
      1948.

1290   Ryan, Ruth Yantzi. "The Expressed Needs of Youth As
       the Basis for a Curriculum Unit in Weekday Reli-
       gious Education." M.A. thesis. University of
       Pittsburgh, 1953.

1291   Schmitt, Marvin J. "I Believe in Weekday Religious
       Education: A Public School Principal States His
       Views." *International Journal of Religious Education*
       27 (February 1951): 11-12.

1292   "Schools and School Districts--Constitutional Law--
       Religious Instruction." *Minnesota Law Review* 11
       (May 1927): 571-72.

1293   Scott, Sarah Corcas. "A Study of the Relationship
       Between Week-Day Church School Attendance and
       Religious Standards." M.A. thesis. University of
       Kansas, 1933.

1294   Seaman,William G. "Gary's Week-Day Community School
       for Religious Instruction." *Religious Education*
       13 (October 1918): 338-42.

1295   Seitz, W. C. "Religious Education in Homogeneous
       School Districts." *Religious Education* 37 (January-
       February 1942): 49-51.

1296   Settle, Myron C. "Weekday Church Schools from Coast
       to Coast." *International Journal of Religious
       Education* 5 (July 1929): 11-12+.

1297   Shaver, Edwin L. "Advice to Weekday Religious Edu-
       cation Workers." *The High School Journal* 31 (May
       1948): 106-11.

1298   ————. "The Legal Situation in Weekday Religious
       Education." *Religious Education* 43 (March-April
       1948): 65-67.

1299   ————. "A Look at Weekday Church Schools." *Reli-
       gious Education* 51 (January 1956): 18-39.

1300   ————. "The Movement for Weekday Religious Edu-
       cation." *Religious Education* 41 (January 1946):
       6-15.

1301 ————. "A New Day Dawns for Weekday Religious Education." International Journal of Religious Education 28 (July 1952): 7-9.

1302 ————. "Weekday Religious Education Is Now on Its Own." International Journal of Religious Education 24 (June 1948): 4-6.

1303 ————. "Weekday Religious Education Today." International Journal of Religious Education 20 (January 1944): 6-7.

1304 ————. "What 'Weekday' Practices Are Legal?" International Journal of Religious Education 37 (March 1961): 22-23+.

1305 Sheeder, Franklin I. "A Denominational Executive Answers Questions About Weekday Education." International Journal of Religious Education 36 (June 1960): 6-7.

1306 Sites, Emri. "Analyzing Difficulties Met in Weekday Schools." International Journal of Religious Education 5 (July 1929): 20-21.

1307 Slaughter, Jim J., Jr. "The Case for Religious Instruction in the Public High School." M.A. thesis. University of Texas (Austin), 1956.

1308 Smith, Charles Clark. "A Study of the Church Bible Schools of Oklahoma in the Light of Principles and Practices of the Public Schools. Ph.D. dissertation. University of Oklahoma, 1935.

1309 Staffeld, Daniel W. "Three Hundred Visits a Year Are Made by Each of the Weekday Teachers in Rochester." International Journal of Religious Education 25 (June 1949): 8-9.

1310 Stetson, P. C. "The Administration of Week-Day Schools of Religious Education." The Elementary School Journal 24 (April 1924): 615-20.

1311 Stout, J. E. "Week-Day Religious Education." The Elementary School Journal 25 (February 1925): 407-09.

1312   Taggart, Esther B. "Weekday Religion in Virginia
       and Texas." M.A. thesis. Southern Methodist
       University, 1947.

1313   Thomas, Audree Madison. "A Proposed Plan for the
       Administration of Week-Day Religious Instruction
       in the Schools of Atlanta." B.D. thesis. Emory
       University, 1928.

1314   Thompson, Kenneth L. "The Status and Trends of Week-
       day Religious Instruction in the High Schools of
       the United States." M.R.E. thesis. Eastern
       Baptist Theological Seminary (Philadelphia), 1938.

1315   Tignor, Robert M. "Growth and Development of a Week-
       Day Religious Education." S.T.M. thesis. Temple
       University, 1936.

1316   Verkuyl, Gerrit. "The Recognition of Outside Reli-
       gious Study by Our Secular Schools." Religious
       Education 5 (June 1910): 136-39.

1317   Washburn, Ellen Frances. "Religious Instruction Can
       Be Introduced Successfully into the Public School
       Curriculum." M.Ed. thesis. Boston College, 1936.

1318   Wasson, Isabel B. "The River Forest Plan of Week-Day
       Religious Education." Religious Education 35
       (October-December 1940): 227-31.

1319   "Weekday Religious Education--A Symposium." Religious
       Education 51 (January 1956): 18-63.

1320   "Weekday Religious Education Today; the Need and Two
       Practical Programs--A Symposium." International
       Journal of Religious Education 15 (March 1939):
       1-12.

1321   "Week-Day Religious Instruction." Religious Educa-
       tion 13 (February 1918): 61-62.

1322   "Week-Day Religious Instruction on Released School
       Time." The Elementary School Journal 34 (November
       1933): 170-73.

1323   "Week-Day Schools of Religion." School and Society
       24 (November 6, 1926): 574-75.

1324 Whittemore, Edward L. "Hawaii's Weekday Classes Stymied." Christian Century 65 (October 13, 1948): 1089-90.

1325 Williams, Horace W. "Week-Day Religious and Moral Instruction." B.D. thesis. Perkins School of Theology, 1923.

1326 Wolcott, Dorothea K. "Weekday Religious Education; Presuppositions, Philosophy, Implications." Religious Education 36 (April 1941): 94-101.

1327 Wood, Clarence A. "Weekday Religious Instruction-- Recent Developments in the Correlation of Bible Study with the Work of the Public Schools: A Survey of Progress." Religious Education 12 (August 1917): 259-64.

1328 Young, T. Basil. "Recent Court Decisions in New York State Affecting Weekday Religious Education." Religious Education 22 (March 1927): 267-73.

1329 Zipperer, Dewey William. "Week-Day Religious Instruction in the United States." M.A. thesis. University of South Carolina, 1925.

CHAPTER 13
CHRISTMAS IN THE SCHOOLS

What should be the role of public schools in the celebration
of the religious dimensions of Christmas? For decades the increasing pluralism of our society has caused school administrators much difficulty in trying to reconcile and balance
opposing opinions.

A federal court ruled in 1980 (Florey v. Sioux Falls School
District, 619F.2d 1311 [8th Circuit]) that schools may include
religious symbolism in Christmas celebrations. The court main-
tained that the holiday was celebrated in order to familiarize
students with their "cultural and religious heritage," not to
inculcate a religious belief. Interestingly, a New York court
ruled the same way in 1959. (See 1343.)

Most of the articles here relate some views of how individ-
ual schools are wrestling with the problem. A distinguished
Protestant theologian urges caution in citation 1334. Citation
1338 reports a survey of 35 states where religious Christmas
observances were found in about one third of school districts.
See also 1340 and 1341. Jewish anguish is well expressed in
1342 and 1345.

See 1348 for a nice newsy overview of the 1980s.

1330   Azneer, J. Leonard. "Religious Holiday Observance
       in Public Schools." Religious Education 55 (July
       1960): 293-96.

1331   Baldwin, Robert F. "Episcopalian Portrays St. Nick
       Over ACLU Objections." Our Sunday Visitor 71
       (December 26, 1982): 3.

1332   Barclay, Dorothy. "Sharing Religious Holidays in
       School." The New York Times Magazine (September 30,
       1962): 62.

1333 Bell, Charles W. "Yule Carol Controversy." New
      York Daily News (December 13, 1981): 11.

1334 Bennett, John C. "When Christmas Becomes Divisive."
      Christianity and Crisis 18 (November 24, 1958):
      162-63.

1335 "Can We Still Sing Christmas Carols in Public Schools?"
      Music Educators Journal 13 (November 1976): 71.

1336 Cavanaugh, A., et al. "Should Schools Recognize
      Certain Religious Holidays When Setting Schedules
      for the School Year?" Michigan Education Journal
      44 (December 1966): 27-32.

1337 "Christmas Curriculum." School and Community 52
      (December 1965): 14-15.

1338 "Christmas in the Schools." NEA Journal 56 (Decem-
      ber 1967): 54-57.

1339 "Christmas Pageantry." Massachusetts Teacher 45
      (December 1965): 12-14.

1340 Culligan, G. "Bah, Humbug, Virginia, We Don't Know:
      Christmas Poses Dilemma for the Schools." American
      Education 3 (December 1966): 14-17.

1341 "Educators Favor Religion in Yule School Programs:
      School Administrators Opinion Poll." The Nation's
      Schools 82 (December 1968): 49.

1342 Forman, B. J. "Are Jewish Children Left Out?"
      Scholastic Arts 57 (December 1957): 25-28.

1343 Garber. Lee Orville. "Christmas Creche May be Placed
      on School Grounds." The Nation's Schools 64 (Decem-
      ber 1959): 82-84.

1344 ————. "Cribs, Creches, and Carols Put Holiday Heat
      on Schools." The Nation's Schools 78 (December
      1966): 44.

1345 "Keep Hanukkah Out of the Public Schools!" Christian
      Century 77 (December 14, 1960): 1462-63.

1346 McCaffrey, Kenneth J. "Hanukkah and Christmas."
      Commonweal 67 (December 13, 1957): 289-90.

1347   "The Meaning of Christmas." The Nation's Schools 58
       (December 1956): 58.

1348   Mouat, Lucia. "Public Schools Face December Dilemma."
       Christian Science Monitor (December 9, 1981): 1.

1349   "On Keeping Christmas." North Carolina Education 32
       (December 1965): 20.

1350   "Opinion Poll--How Should the Public Schools Celebrate
       Holidays or Should They? Superintendents Disagree
       on the Answer." The Nation's Schools 59 (February
       1957): 92, 94.

1351   Powell, O. et al. "Christmas and the Public Schools."
       The Instructor 77 (December 1967): 16-18.

1352   Sherwin, J. S. "Christmas in the Schools." School
       and Society 85 (November 9, 1957): 331-33.

1353   "Should Schools Recognize Certain Religious Holidays
       When Setting Schedules for the School Year?" Michigan
       Education Journal 45 (December 1966): 27-32.

1354   "Tinsel and Trouble: Annual Battle Over Christmas
       Observances Mar Holiday." Church & State 36 (February
       1983): 11-12.

1355   Yeomans, Edward. "The Approach to Christmas." Pro-
       gressive Education 7 (December 1930): 379-82.

CHAPTER 14
BACCALAUREATES AND DEVOTIONALS

Devotional exercises and religious services at graduations
(called baccalaureates) were often divisive and led to intense
community tension. No major court decisions with national
implications were rendered against the practice, but the
ecumenical movement and a heightened awareness of religious
diversity have just about ended these problems today (except
in recalcitrant Georgia, see 1358).

1356 Boyer, William W. "Baccalaureate in Broadhead: A
      Study in Interfaith Tension." School and Society
      88 (April 9, 1960): 183-86.

1357 Crockett, Wilbury A. "Worship in a High School."
      International Journal of Religious Education 27
      (November 1950): 10-11.

1358 Galloway, Jim. "Georgia Schools Make Religion the
      Fourth R." Atlanta Journal and Constitution
      (March 25, 1984): 14A.

1359 Garber, Lee Orville. "Court Defends 'Under God'
      in Pledge of Allegiance." Nation's Schools 60
      (August 1957): 50-53.

1360 ———. "Display of Ten Commandments, Saying Grace,
      Ruled Illegal." Nation's Schools 60 (December 1957):
      45-46.

1361 Gummere, J. F. "Schools, Songs, and Supplications."
      School and Society 98 (Summer 1970): 299-330.

1362 Howard, J. Gordon. "Easter Week in a Public High
      School." International Journal of Religious Edu-
      cation 8 (February 1932): 18+.

1363 Kerlinger, Fred N. "Religious Displays and Public
      Education." School and Society 90 (April 21, 1962):
      196-98.

1364 Konrad, A. G. "Baccalaureate Services in the Schools." The Education Digest 32 (September 1966): 41-43.

1365 ———. "Relinquish Baccalaureate Services." Journal of Secondary Education 41 (April 1966): 180-85.

1366 Meek, Charles S. "Public Schools--Religious Exercises." National Corporation Reporter (October 1910): 253-54.

1367 "Morning Devotional Period in Schools." School and Society 94 (March 19, 1966): 145.

1368 "Religious Exercises and the Public Schools." Arkansas Law Review 20 (Winter 1967): 320+.

1369 Sheffey, E. Summers. "The First Amendment and Distribution of Religious Literature in the Public Schools." Virginia Law Review 41 (October 1955): 789-807.

CHAPTER 15
EQUAL ACCESS: NEW CONFLICT FOR THE EIGHTIES

Can religious groups use public school facilities for worship, prayer, discussion and proselytizing? Should the schools
accommodate those students who wish to engage in "student-
initiated" and "wholly voluntary" religious activities on
campus? This issue, now called "equal access" by proponents,
is so new that articles are just beginning to appear. As
courts and the Congress grapple with its implications, the
literature will undoubtedly increase.

Toms and Whitehead (1376, 1376b) are advocates of more
religious expression in the schools. The editors of Church &
State have been more critical (1370, 1370a, 1371, 1374).
Whitehead is one of the intellectual guns of the Religious
Right.

1370 Buie, Jim. "A Season of Prayer." Church & State 37
      (May 1984): 6-7.

1370a Buie, Jim. "Equal Access Derailed." Church & State
      37 (June 1984): 9-11.

1371 Conn, Joseph L. "Targeting the Schools." Church &
      State 36 (January 1983): 14-16.

1371a Dewar, Heather. "Dade Takes Lead in Opposing School
      Prayer Bill." Miami News (May 19, 1984).

1372 Drakeman, Donald L. "Religion's Place in the Public
      Schools." Christian Century 101 (May 2, 1984):
      462-463.

1373 Howell, Leon. "Equal Access in the Public Schools."
      Christian Century 101 (May 9, 1984): 477-78.

1374 Menendez, Albert J. "Voluntary School Prayer: Is
      the Hatfield Bill the Real McCoy?" Church & State
      36 (May 1983): 6-8.

1375   "Should Congress Enact Equal Access?" <u>Church &
          State</u> 37 (May 1984): 8-9.

1376   Toms, Robert L. and Whitehead, John W. "The Religious
          Student in Public Education: Resolving a Consti-
          tutional Dilemma." <u>Emory Law Journal</u> 27 (Winter
          1978): 30-44.

1376a Ungar, Barry. "Equal Access Isn't Equal Access."
          <u>Philadelphia Inquirer</u> (May 15, 1984).

1376b Whitehead, John W. <u>The Freedom of Religious Ex-
          pression in the Public High Schools</u>. Westchester,
          Illinois: Crossway Books, 1983.

CHAPTER 16
RELIGION AND THE TEACHER

What should a teacher do if a student asks about the teacher's religious beliefs? If the teacher is a fervent believer in some religion, does this pose potential problems in a classroom situation? Is the teacher obligated, out of a sense of fairness, to remain scrupulously neutral? These and similar questions are touched upon in this chapter.

A conservative Protestant view is expressed in 1377 by a spokesperson for an organization committed to getting more religion of an evangelical variety in the classroom. A similar viewpoint is found in 1384 and 1387. Catholic views are expressed in 1378, 1391, 1393 and 1395.

How are teacher views on religion formed? See 1381, 1382, 1388 and 1398.

1377 Adams, Marjorie E., ed. God in the Classroom. South Pasadena: National Educators Fellowship, 1970.

1378 Browne, Henry J. "Public Schools and the Catholic." Commonweal 77 (January 25, 1963): 455-57.

1379 Chamberlin, J. Gordon. "The Dilemma of the Christian Teacher." Teachers College Record 54 (October 1952): 38-42.

1380 Cole, Stewart G. "The Dilemma of the Public School Educator." Religious Education 58 (Mary 1958): 158-65.

1381 Crouch, Hugh C. "Religious Education in Certain Tax-Supported, Teacher Education Institutions." M.A. thesis. Western Illinois State College (Macomb, Illinois), 1956.

1382 Dawson, Eugene E. "Religion in Teacher Education." Religious Education 50 (July 1955): 238-42.

1383   Eglin, Paula Garrison. "Creationism vs. Evolution:
       A Study of the Opinions of Georgia Science Teachers."
       Ph.D. dissertation. Georgia State University, 1983.

1384   Hall, Christopher. The Christian Teacher and the Law.
       Oak Park, Illinois: Christian Legal Society, 1975.

1385   Hill, W. O. "The Teacher and Religious Exercises."
       Education 85 (May 1965): 562-66.

1386   Hubner, Sister Mary. Professional Attitudes Toward
       Religion in the Public Schools of the U. S. since
       1900. Washington, D.C.: Catholic University of
       America, 1944.

1387   Jerome, Hattie Louise. "The Spiritual Influence of
       the Teacher." Education 15 (May 1895): 560-61.

1388   Kilpatrick, Harold. "Texas Teachers in Religious
       Retraining." National Council Outlook 9 (May 1959):
       20-21.

1389   King, Lauren Alfred. "How Far: Not Whether but How;
       the Teacher's Religious Opinions in the Classroom."
       Journal of Higher Education 26 (October 1955):
       361-65.

1390   Lau, Donald A. "Value Patterns of Elementary School
       Teachers in Relation to Attitudes Expressed Toward
       Religious Issues in the Classroom." Ed.D. disser-
       tation. Syracuse University, 1970.

1391   McCabe, Bernard. "Catholic Teachers in Public
       Schools." America 79 (August 7, 1948): 407-08.

1392   Menkis, B. "Evangelical Responsibility in Public
       Education." Christianity Today 15 (February 12,
       1971): 10-12.

1393   O"Neill, James M. The Catholic in Secular Education.
       New York: Longmans Green, 1956.

1394   Parker, Cleon G. "The Teacher and Current Proposals
       for Dealing with Religion in the Public School."
       M.A. thesis. Phillips University, 1954.

1395 Quigley, A.E. "Catholic Teachers in Public Schools;
      How Much Do a Teacher's Religious Convictions Affect
      Her Work in the Classroom?" Commonweal 31 (March 8,
      1940): 426-28.

1396 Sebaly, A.L. "The AACTE Teacher Education Religion
      Project at Mid-Passage." Religious Education 51
      (July 1956): 266-69.

1397 ———. "A Five Year Study of Teacher Education and
      Religion." Phi Delta Kappan 40 (May 1959): 314-17.

1398 ———. ed. Teacher Education and Religion. Oneonta,
      New York: The American Association of Colleges
      for Teacher Education, 1959.

1399 Sewell, E. G. "The Christian Teacher in the Public
      Schools." Journal of Arkansas Education 36 (Dec-
      ember 1963): 11+.

1400 Trepp, Leo. "A Report on Teacher Attitudes Regarding
      Moral and Spiritual Values in Public Education."
      Religious Education 48 (May 1953): 166-68.

1401 Van Houten, E. M. "On Being a Real Teacher; Religion
      in the Classroom." New York State Education 33
      (April 1946): 557-59.

1402 Williams, Erma Polly. "The Role of the Christian
      Public School Teacher in the State of New Jersey."
      M.R.E. thesis. Princeton Theological Seminary,
      1960.

CHAPTER 17
RELIGIOUS ELEMENTS IN TEXTBOOKS

Religious elements in textbooks are often significant and determinative. Previous studies (see especially 1406, 1413, 1414, 1417, 1426) demonstrate the importance of treating religion seriously and objectively. Many texts did not meet those standards but were biased and prejudiced against religious minorities.

For a modern, open-minded approach see 1425. For the recent conflict over creationism see 1405, 1411, 1412 and 1430.

1403   Alilunas, Leo J. "Ethnocentrism in Public and Parochial School American History Textbooks." Religious Education 60 (March 1965): 83-89.

1404   Ayers, Milas McCord. "Religious Content of Frequently Used Undergraduate Professional Education Textbooks." Ed.D. dissertation. George Peabody College of Teachers, 1958.

1405   Bird, Wendell R. "Freedom of Religion and Science Instruction in Public Schools." Yale Law Journal 87 (January 1978): 515-38.

1406   Blocker, Richard Daniel. "Religious Content in State-Approved Textbooks Used in American Public Secondary Schools in the Fields of Language Arts, Mathematics, Science and Social Studies During the Year 1966." Ph.D. dissertation. American University, 1968.

1407   Bocklage, Sister Georgine. "A Comparative Study of American History Textbooks Widely Used in Parochial and Public Schools." M.Ed. thesis. St. Louis University, 1951.

1408   Bowlin, Ruth E. "Relation of Science and Religion as It Pertains to the Teaching of General Science in High School." M.R.E. thesis. Biblical Seminary in New York, 1945.

1409 Bundy, Leon Francis Ethelbert. "The Emphasis on
      Religion in Courses of Study; the Relative Space
      Given to Religion in Courses of Study in the Field
      of the Social Studies in Grades 7 to 12 Inclusive."
      M.S. thesis. Syracuse University, 1938.

1410 Byrd, Oliver Erasmus. "Religion and the School Health
      Program." California Journal of Secondary Edu-
      cation 30 (February 1955): 66-69.

1411 Crawford, Gary E. "Keeping Schools Neutral." Church
      & State 35 (April 1982): 20-21.

1412 "Creationism, Evolution and the Schools." Church &
      State 34 (May 1981): 12-14.

1413 Dawson, John Harper. "A Survey of the Religious
      Content of American World History Textbooks Written
      Prior to 1900." Ph.D. dissertation. University
      of Pittsburgh, 1954.

1414 Elson, Ruth Miller. Guardians of Tradition: American
      Schoolbooks of the Nineteenth Century. Lincoln:
      University of Nebraska Press, 1964.

1415 Howley, Mary Catherine. "The Treatment of Religion
      in American History Textbooks for Grades Seven and
      Eight from 1783 to 1956. Ed.D. dissertation.
      Columbia University, 1959.

1416 McCausland, James Harold. "Religious Content of the
      Basic Social Science Textbooks in the Secondary
      Schools of Three Pennsylvania Public School
      Districts." M.A. thesis. University of Pitts-
      burgh, 1948.

1417 McDevitt, Philip R. "How Bigotry Was Kept Alive by
      Old-Time Textbooks." American Catholic Historical
      Society of Philadelphia Records 24 (September 1913):
      251-61.

1418 McMillan, Richard Cupp. "Religious Content in
      Selected Social Studies Textbooks." Ph.D. disser-
      tation. Duke University, 1970.

1419 Nietz, John A. "Some Findings from Analyses of Old
      Textbooks." History of Education Journal 3 (Spring
      1952): 79-87.

1420 Pezynska, Sister M. Accursia. "The Treatment of
      Catholicism in American Histories of Education,
      1900-1950. Ph.D. dissertation. Fordham Univer-
      sity, 1965.

1421 Pflug, Harold. "Religion in Missouri Textbooks."
      Phi Delta Kappan 36 (April 1955): 258-60.

1422 ————. "Theistic Religion in Missouri Public School
      Textbooks." Ph.D. dissertation. Yale University,
      1950.

1423 Pletcher, Inez Calhoun. "Religious Content in
      Virginia High School Literature Textbooks." M.A.
      thesis. University of Pittsburgh, 1952.

1424 Shankland, Rebecca H. "The McGuffey Readers and
      Moral Education." Harvard Educational Review 31
      (Winter 1961): 60-72.

1425 Shaver, J. P. "Diversity, Violence, and Religion:
      Textbooks in a Pluralistic Society." The School
      Review 75 (Autumn 1967): 311-28.

1426 Tingelstad, Oscar A. Religious Element in American
      School Readers to 1850. Chicago: 1925.

1427 Vinie, Earl. "The Treatment of Religious Freedom
      and Other Religious Content in American History
      Schoolbooks." Ph.D. dissertation. Yale Univer-
      sity, 1929.

1428 Warren, Harold C. "Changing Conceptions in the
      Religious Elements in Early American School Readers."
      Ph.D. dissertation. University of Pittsburgh, 1951.

1429 Wilson, Karl K. "Historical Survey of the Religious
      Content of American Geography Textbooks from 1874
      to 1895." Ph.D. dissertation. University of
      Pittsburgh, 1951.

1430 Wood, James E., Jr. "Scientific Creationism and the
      Public Schools." Journal of Church and State 24
      (Spring 1982): 231-44.

CHAPTER 18
ARE PUBLIC SCHOOLS GODLESS?

The inevitable secularization of public education, stemming partially from the increasing religious pluralism of our society, has led to intense debate, usually from critics of the trend. See 1456, 1457, 1459, 1466, 1467, 1478, 1489, 1507, 1508, 1513, 1515.

Roman Catholics were critics of both the Protestant orientation of some schools (1431, 1465) and also of the secularizing tendencies (1433-1446, 1447, 1448, 1455, 1477, 1502).

Protestants were generally wont to defend public education as essentially moral (1451, 1452, 1458, 1470, 1471, 1472, 1485, 1488, 1497, 1500, 1516) and blasted Catholic critics for alleged hidden agendas (1475, 1490, 1492, 1493).

For an analysis of conservative Protestant dissatisfaction today see 1461, 1483, 1486, 1496, 1514.

1431 "Are Public Schools Protestant?" America 82 (March 4, 1950): 627-28.

1432 Blakely, Paul L. "American Spirit in Education; Ancient Ordinance for Godly Living.", America 55 (July 4, 1936): 297-98.

1433 ————. "An Important School Decision." America 35 (May 8, 1926): 88-89.

1434 ————. "Can the Public Schools Be Reformed?" America 37 (June 25, 1927): 256-57.

1435 ————. "Can the Public Schools Endure?" America 50 (November 18, 1933): 157-58.

1436 ————. "Catholics and the Public Schools." America 37 (May 28, 1927): 158-59.

1437 ———. "Christ in the Schools." America 40
     (December 29, 1928): 284-85.

1438 ———. "Do We Criticize the Public School?"
     America 38 (February 11, 1928): 440-41.

1439 ———. "Little Flock Without a Shepherd; State
     Education Need Not Be Irreligious." America 56
     (October 17, 1936): 33-34.

1440 ———. "The Nation's Fictitious Cornerstone."
     America 37 (May 7, 1927): 88-89.

1441 ———. "The Public Schools and Religion." America
     37 (June 18, 1927): 231-31.

1442 ———. "Religious Illiteracy in the Public Schools."
     America 62 (February 24, 1940): 541.

1443 ———. "Rights of the State in Education." America
     42 (February 1, 1930): 409-10.

1444 ———. "School Bus for the Privileged." America
     68 (January 9, 1943): 372-73.

1445 ———. "Schools and the Law." America 63 (June 8,
     1940): 230-31.

1446 ———. "Spartan Training in the Schools of Chicago;
     Fear Is a Feebler Motive Than Morality and Religion."
     America 59 (August 20, 1938): 464-65.

1447 Butler, William J. "No Lamb of God in School."
     Catholic World 167 (June 1948): 203-11.

1448 Canavan, Francis P. "The State as Educator." Thought
     25 (September 1950): 487-96.

1449 Caswell, Hollis L. "Are the Public Schools Irreligious?"
     Teachers College Record 54 (April 1953): 357-65.

1450 "Catholic Citizens and Public Education." Catholic
     World 76 (January 1903): 430-35.

1451 "The Church and Public Schools." International Jour-
     nal of Religious Education 34 (May 1958): 3-52.

1452   "The Church and the Public School in Religious
       Education." Religious Education 10 (December
       1915): 566-74.

1453   "Churches and the Public Schools." International
       Journal of Religious Education 40 (September 1963):
       22-23.

1454   Coester, Donald Frank. "The Responsibility and
       Obligations of the Church in Relation to Public
       Education." S.T.M. thesis. Lutheran Theological
       Seminary (Philadelphia), 1958.

1455   Confrey, Burton. Secularism in American Education--
       Its History. Washington, D.C.: Catholic University
       of America, 1931.

1456   Coogan, J. E. "That Wall of Separation and the Public
       School." Catholic World 172 (January 1951): 252-55.

1457   Cordaro, Joseph A. "The Evolution of Secularism in
       the Public Schools." M.S. thesis. Northern
       Illinois University, 1953.

1458   Cubberley, Ellwood P. "Battle to Eliminate Sectar-
       ianism in the Public Schools." NEA Journal 41
       (April 1952): 228-30.

1459   Curran, Francis Xavier. "The Churches and the Schools:
       American Protestantism and Popular Elementary Edu-
       cation." Ph.D. dissertation. Columbia University,
       1951.

1460   Curry, B. L. "How Godless is Public Education?"
       Kentucky School Journal 22 (February 1944): 43-44.

1461   Davis, Harold. "Dealing with Religious Differences."
       The National Elementary Principal 37 (September
       1957): 83-87.

1462   DeBoer, Ray L. "Historical Study of Mormon Education
       and the Influence of Its Philosophy on Public
       Education in Utah." Ph.D. dissertation. University
       of Denver, 1952.

1463   Dierenfield, Richard B. "Extent of Religious Influence
       in American Public Schools." Religious Education
       56 (May 1962): 173-179+.

1464 Diffley, Jerome E. "Catholic Reaction to American
      Public Education, 1792-1852." Ph.D. dissertation.
      University of Notre Dame, 1959.

1465 Dunn, William K. "The Decline of the Teaching of
      Religion in the American Public Elementary School
      in the States, Originally the Thirteen Colonies,
      1776-1861." Ph.D. dissertation. Johns Hopkins
      University, 1956.

1466 ————. What Happened to Religious Education?
      Baltimore: Johns Hopkins University Press, 1958.

1467 Edidin, Ben M. "Jewish Attitude Toward Religion in
      Schools." The Nation's Schools 40 (September 1947):
      23-24.

1468 Erickson, Donald A. "Religious Consequences of Public
      and Sectarian Schooling." The School Review 72
      (Spring 1964): 22-33.

1469 Fleming, W. S. God in Our Public Schools. Pittsburgh:
      National Reform Association, 1942.

1470 ————. "Keep the School Door Open to Religion."
      The Nation's Schools 36 (December 1945): 50-51.

1471 Gibbons, Ray. "Protestantism and Public Education."
      Social Action 15 (February 15, 1949): 4-27.

1472 Gilbert, Arthur. "Major Problems Facing Schools in
      a Pluralistic Society." Theory Into Practice 4
      (February 1965): 23-28.

1473 ————. "Religion in the Public School: A New
      Approach to the Jewish Position." Religious Edu-
      cation 56 (July 1961): 297-301+.

1474 Harcourt, Richard. The Great Conspiracy Against Our
      American Public Schools. San Francisco: California
      News Company, 1890.

1475 Hicks, R. S. "Our Schools, Are They Godless?"
      California Journal of Secondary Education 23
      (March 1948): 160-63.

1476 Hogan, G. Stuart. "Underprivileged Children of the Public Schools." Catholic Mind 38 (April 8, 1940): 126-37.

1477 Huff, A. LeRoy. "The Change from the Religious to the Secular Aim in Elementary Education." Religious Education 22 (March 1927): 231-36.

1478 Hunt, Herold C. "Are Public Schools Godless?" School Executive 71 (May 1952): 19-22.

1479 Jenkinson, Edward. "Is Secular Humanism Being Taught in Our Public Schools?" Church & State 36 (May 1983): 21-22.

1480 Jones, Attwood Jason, Jr. "Southern Baptist Attitudes Toward Church-State Cooperation in Religious Instruction, 1930-1952." Th.D. dissertation. Southwestern Baptist Theological Seminary, 1957.

1481 Jorgenson, Lloyd P. "The Birth of a Tradition: Historical Origins of Non-Sectarian Public Schools." Phi Delta Kappan 44 (June 1963): 407-14.

1482 LaHaye, Tim. The Battle for the School. Old Tappan, New Jersey: Revell, 1983.

1483 Leibson, Bernard. "The Public Schools: Are They 'Godless' or Ethical?" Clearing House 27 (September 1952): 3-7.

1484 Lynn, Robert W. "The Public Schools and Protestant Faith." Social Action 19 (December 1952): 2-29.

1485 Martin, Renwick H. Our Public Schools--Christian or Secular? Pittsburgh: The National Reform Association, 1962.

1486 Mater, Milton. "The Vestige of God." Commonweal 52 (April 14, 1950): 11-15.

1487 Mayo, Amory Dwight. Religion in the Common Schools. Cincinnati: R. Clarke & Co., 1869.

1488 McCasland, S. Vernon. "Our Secularized Education." Christian Century 58 (December 17, 1941): 1576-78.

1489 Mead, Edwin D. The Roman Catholic Church and the
      Public Schools. Boston: George H. Ellis, 1890.

1490 Merrill, A. W. "Causes of Friction Between State
      and Church in the Field of Religious Education."
      Religious Education 22 (June 1927): 560-63.

1491 Meyer, Agnes E. "The Public School and Sectarian
      Religion." The Educational Forum 12 (May 1948):
      435-50.

1492 ————. "Shall the Churches Invade the Schools?"
      Reader's Digest 52 (March 1948): 65-69.

1493 Milligan, John P. "Think on These Things When You
      Hear Someone Say the Schools Are Godless." NEA
      Journal 41 (December 1952): 587.

1494 Moehlman, Arthur B. "Schools Are Not Godless."
      The Nation's Schools 28 (November 1941): 14.

1495 Moore, Opal. Why Johnny Can't Learn. Milford,
      Michigan: Mott Media, 1975.

1496 Nelson, Claud. "Public Education and Protestant
      Consensus." Christianity and Crisis 19 (September
      21, 1959): 130-32.

1497 Novak, Michael. "Religion in the Public Schools;
      Catholic Children at Least Can Lose Their Faith."
      The New Republic 148 (April 13, 1963): 16-18.

1498 Page, Ann L. and Clelland, Donald A. "The Kanawha
      County Textbook Controversy." Social Forces 57
      (1978): 265-81.

1499 Pierce, D. J. "Parents' Rights in Public Education."
      America 84 (March 31, 1951): 747-49.

1500 Rogers, Virgil M. "Are the Public Schools Godless?"
      Christian Century 74 (September 11, 1957): 1065-67.

1501 Scharper, Philip. "Catholics and Public Schools."
      Commonweal 79 (January 31, 1964): 533-38.

1502 Schwickerath, R. "Fatal Error in Education and Its
      Remedy." American Catholic Quarterly 28 (October
      1903): 756-79.

1503 Shaver, Erwin L. "Religion and the Public Schools--
      Trends in Protestant Thinking." Religious Edu-
      cation 44 (November 1949): 332-35.

1504 Sherman, F. "Lutheran Theological Perspective on the
      Public Schools." Religious Education 56 (November
      1962: 431-440.

1505 Smith, B. Othanel. "Let's Make the Sectarian Issue
      Clear." Progressive Education 26 (February 1949):
      97-98.

1506 ———. "What Do the Sectarians Want?" Progressive
      Education 26 (February 1949): 121-24.

1507 Smith, C. B. "Keeping Public Schools Secular." The
      Educational Forum 29 (November 1964): 71-77.

1508 Smith, Charles Bunyan. "American Public Schools Must
      Remain Secular." Journal of Teacher Education 8
      (June 1957): 201-06.

1509 Smith, Furman. "Surrender to Caesar?" America 107
      (July 14, 1962): 494-95.

1510 Smith, Gerald B. "Attitudes of the Churches as to
      the Respective Spheres of Church and State in the
      Matter of Religious Education." Religious Edu-
      cation 22 (April 1927): 345-67.

1511 Smith, William Cooke. "The Mormons as a Factor in
      the Development of the Public School System of
      Arizona." M.A. thesis. Brigham Young University,
      1929.

1512 Stiles, Gerald Johnston. "Evangelicals and Public
      Education." Ed.D. dissertation. Virginia Poly-
      technic Institute, 1980.

1513 Thayer, V. T. The Attack upon the American Secular
      School. Boston: Beacon, 1951.

1514 Towns, Elmer Leon. Have the Public Schools Had It?
      Nashville: Thomas Nelson, 1974.

1515 Weigle, Luther A. "The Secularization of Public Edu-
      cation." Religious Education 21 (February 1926):
      90-95.

1516 Williams, John Paul. "Protestantism and Public Education." Christian Century 64 (March 12, 1947): 330-31.

1517 Wilson, Bryan R. "Sectarians and Schooling." The School Review 72 (Spring 1964): 1-12.

CHAPTER 19
THE CATHOLIC PUBLIC SCHOOL

In many predominantly Catholic rural communities, a unique
hybrid type of school system developed in this century: a
combination Catholic-public school. For all practical purposes
the school functioned as a parochial school, complete with
catechism classes and religious worship. The few non-Catholic
students were expected to accept the situation.

Many non-Catholics refused to do so, instead bringing suit,
beginning with the Dixon case in New Mexico in 1948, to stop
the situation. The existence of these schools harmed Catholic-
Protestant relations in many communities, especially in Ohio,
Kentucky, Indiana and Missouri. Today they are things of the
past.

Controversialists like Paul Blanshard (1518) and Dale
Francis (1525) conducted a verbal war over captive schools
and related topics during the Protestant-Catholic Cold War
that lasted from the end of World War II until the end of the
Kennedy presidency.

1518   Blanshard, Paul. "The State and Catholic Power in
         the United States." Hibbert Journal 52 (April 1954):
         231-39.

1519   "Catholicism and Public Schools in New Mexico." Utah
         Law Review 3 (Fall 1953): 467-80.

1520   Chambers, Merritt Madison. "When Is a School Sec-
         tarian?" Nation's Schools 29 (February 1942):
         53-54.

1521   Clancy, William. "Paul Blanshard Returns to His
         Subject." The New Republic 142 (February 1960):
         16-18.

1522   Dawson, Joseph Martin. "Public Schools, Catholic
         Model." Christian Century 65 (June 23, 1948): 627-29.

1523 Dorchester, Daniel. Romanism Versus the Public School System. New York: Phillips and Hunt, 1888.

1524 Dunn, James B. The Pope's Last Veto in American Politics. Boston: Committee of One Hundred, 1890.

1525 Francis, Dale. "Bigotry in Action." Sign 34 (March 1955): 17-19.

1526 ————. "Who is Paul Blanshard?" Catholic Digest 14 (May 1950): 36-41.

1527 Garber, Lee Orville. "May Public and Parochial School Authorities Maintain a Single School System?" The Nation's Schools 53 (June 1954): 61-62.

1528 ————. "Supreme Court Defines Church-State Separation for Public Schools in New Mexico." The Nation's Schools 49 (February 1952): 69-72.

1529 Heffron, Edward J. "Protestant-Catholic Tensions." Catholic Digest 13 (February 1949): 61-66.

1530 Jacobson, Philip. "The Nonsectarian Public Parochial School." Christian Century 86 (June 4, 1969): 769-74.

1531 Johnson, Willard. "Whose Country is This? Notes on Protestant-Roman Catholic Relationships." Christendom 12 (Autumn 1947): 507-14.

1532 Murray, John Courtney. "Paul Blanshard and the New Nativism." The Month 5 (New Series) (April 1951): 214-25.

1533 Nations, Gilbert O. Roman Catholic War on Public Schools. Washington, D.C.: Independent Publishing Company, 1931.

1534 "New Mexico Court Upholds Dixon School Decision." Christian Century 68 (October 10, 1951): 1149-50.

1535 "New Mexico School Case Opens." Christian Century 65 (October 13, 1948): 1067-68.

1536 Ralph, Sister Mary. "The Organization and Development of Catholic Public Schools in Clinton County." M.A. thesis. De Paul University, 1949.

1537 Robinson, Allyn P. "A Protestant Looks at the Catholic Threat." Catholic Mind 56 (November-December 1958): 485-95.

1538 Sanders, Tom G. "Protestantism, Catholicism and POAU." Christianity and Crisis 17 (September 16, 1957): 115-18.

1539 Schuster, George N. "The Catholic Controversy." Harpers 199 (November 1949): 25-32.

1540 Selekman, Sylvia Kopald. "A Wave of the Past: Lessons of the Anti-Catholic Movement in the United States." Menorah Journal 31 (January 1943): 18-33.

1541 Weigel, Gustave. "Catholic and Protestant: End of War?" Thought 33 (Autumn 1958): 383-387.

CHAPTER 20
RELIGIOUS GARB IN THE CLASSROOM

Closely related to the captive school was the religious
garb controversy in about a dozen states that began around
1900 and died out around 1960. Interesting educational and
religious liberty implications were raised by this issue. See
1542, 1544 and 1546.

The issue reappeared in 1984 when an Oregon adherent of the
Sikh religion was fired from a public school teaching post.
(See 1552.)

1542   American Law Reports Annotated. "Wearing of Religious
       Garb by Public-School Teachers." 60 ALR 2nd (1958):
       300-07.

1543   Armstrong, C. A. "What Happened in North Dakota?"
       Christian Century 65 (July 28, 1948): 754-55.

1544   Blum, Virgil C. "Religious Liberty and the Religious
       Garb." University of Chicago Law Review 22 (Summer
       1955): 875-88.

1545   Boyer, William W. Jr. "Sectarian Teachers in Wiscon-
       sin Public Schools: A Study in Administrative
       Decision Making." Religious Education 57 (May 1962):
       195-202+.

1546   Fitzsimons, Simon. "Are Religious Garb Decisions
       Constitutional?" The Catholic World 75 (August
       1902); 567-80.

1547   Garber, Lee Orville. "If Nuns Teach in Public School,
       Kentucky Court Ruling Permits Them to Wear Religious
       Garb." The Nation's Schools 59 (March 1957): 81-82.

1548   Gorman, Ashley. " . . . Teachers Wearing Religious
       Garb." Wayne Law Review 3 (Winter 1956): 57-62.
       Notes.

1549 Hall, Donald M. " . . . Members of Religious Orders
      as Teachers in Public Schools." Tulane Law Review
      31 (June 1957): 676-79.

1550 McEachern, Margaret. "Nuns Carry on in North Dakota."
      Catholic Digest 13 (March 1949): 93-96.

1551 McGee, Sister Clare Mary. "The Causes and Effects
      of the 'Dixon Case.'" M.A. thesis. Catholic
      University of America, 1955.

1552 Menendez, Albert J. "Kicking the Habit." Church &
      State 37 (May 1984): 12-13.

1553 Patrick, T. L. "Is Garb Sectarian?" The Educational
      Forum 34 (March 1970): 353-58.

1554 Pawlowski, Joseph T. "Validity of Salary Payments
      to Teachers Wearing Religious Garb While Teaching."
      Notre Dame Lawyer 16 (January 1941): 148-50.

1555 Philibert, Sister M. "Nuns in New Mexico's Public
      Schools." America 80 (November 27, 1948): 207-08.

1556 "Religious Garb in the Public Schools: A Study in
      Conflicting Liberties." University of Chicago Law
      Review 22 (Summer 1955): 888-95.

1557 "Unusual but Not Unprecedented, Bishop Muench Says
      of Secular Dress Used by Nun-Teachers." Catholic
      Educational Review 47 (February 1949): 132-33.

CHAPTER 21
OTHER BIBLIOGRAPHIES

A few previous bibliographies are recommended. Drouin and Flowers are very helpful. Little is especially good for pamphlets, dissertations, and church pronouncements.

1558 Blakeman, Edward W. "A Bibliography--Religious Education and the Public Schools." Religious Education 43 (January 1948): 42-50.

1559 Boehm, C. H. "Religion and Public Education in the United States: Bibliographical Essay." American Review 3 (Spring 1964): 56-70.

1560 Brickman, William W. "Educational Literature Review: Religion and Education." School and Society 67 (March 27, 1948): 245-53.

1561 Drouin, Edmond G. The School Question: A Bibliography on Church-State Relationships in American Education, 1940-1960. Washington, D.C.: Catholic University of America, 1963.

1562 Flowers, Ronald B. "A Selected Bibliography on Religion and Public Education." Journal of Church and State 14 (Autumn 1972): 475-505.

1563 Little, Lawrence Calvin. Religion and Public Education; A Bibliography. Pittsburgh: University of Pittsburgh, 1966. (Revised Edition: 1968.)

1564 ————. "Selected Bibliography." Religious Education 44 (May 1949): 177-80.

1565 ————. "A Selected Bibliography on Religion and Public Education." Religious Education 46 (July 1951): 251-56.

1566 Politella, Joseph. Religion in Education: An Annotated Bibliography. New York: Oneonta, 1956.

AUTHOR INDEX

156

Author Index

Blashfield, Herbert W. 30
Blocker, Richard Daniel 1406
Blum, Virgil C. 1544
Bocklage, Sister Georgine 1407
Bodden, Rosalind V. 1068
Boddy, William H. 1038
Bode, Boyd Henry 31
Boehm, C. H. 637, 1559
Boehme, Galen Ray 962
Boger, David A. 32
Boles, Donald E. 33-34
Bolmeier, Edward Claude 1219
Boone, R. G. 1039
Borowski, Maria C. R. 1069
Bortner, Ross L. 478
Bouton, Eugene 35, 479
Boutwell, W. D. 1040
Bower, William C. 36-37, 480-
  481, 963, 1070
Bowlin, Ruth E. 1408
Boyer, William W. 868, 1071,
  1356, 1545
Boyle, Robert Driscoll 1041
Bozell, L. Brent 638
Bracler, J. F. 1042
Bradshaw, Emerson O. 38
Bradshaw, L. A. 869
Braiterman, Marvin 39
Brant, Irving 639
Breig, Joseph A. 482
Bremeld, Theodore 483
Brickman, Benjamin 40
Brickman, William W. 41-42,
  617, 640, 822-824
Briles, Charles W. 1043
Brislawn, Maurice John 43
Broden, Thomas F. 1072
Broudy, Harry S. 484
Brouillette, Eloise Norma 485
Brown, Betty 44
Brown, Elmer E. 45
Brown, E. H. 1044
Brown, Ernest J. 641
Brown, Francis J. 46
Brown, Samuel Windsor 618
Brubacher, John S. 486-488,
  1220

Bruce, Homer L., Jr. 1073
Buchanan, G. Sidney 825
Bucher, Charles A. 47
Buddy, Charles F. 826
Buie, Jim 835, 1370, 1370a
Bundy, Leon Francis Ethelbert
  1409
Burrows, Albert H. 48
Bussert, Martha Lucille 964
Butler, Harris D., Jr. 49
Butler, William J. 642-643,
  1447
Butts, R. Freeman 50-51
Buzzard, Lynn R. 52
Byrd, Oliver Erasmus 1410
Byrnes, Lawrence 53

Cabot, Ella Lyman 489
Cahn, Edmond 644
Calhoun, P. 645
Campbell, Sister Margaret 1221
Canavan, Francis P. 800, 1448
Carmichael, A. Max 55
Carpenter, William Weston 490,
  1074
Carr, William G. 491
Caswell, Hollis L. 1449
Cates, E. E. 870
Cavanaugh, A. 1336
Cavert, Walter D. 1075-1076
Chace, Elizabeth B. 492
Chaffee, Charles E. 1222
Chamberlin, J. Gordon 1379
Chambers, Merritt Madison 1520
Chandler, C. C. 56
Charters, W. W. 57
Cheever, George B. 871
Childs, John L. 493
Chipkin, Israel S. 58-59
Choper, Jesse H. 646
Ciarlo, Enrico L. 61
Clancy, William 1521
Clark, Rufus W. 872
Clark, Samuel I. 62
Clarke, James Ratcliffe 63
Cleary, Catherine B. 827
Clifford, J. 494

SUBJECT INDEX

Alabama 880
Arizona 1511

California 172, 584, 589, 599, 856, 1048, 1209
Catholics 236, 358, 366, 437, 751, 761-763, 875, 916, 951,
    995, 1079-1080, 1145-1146, 1206, 1225, 1266, 1378, 1391,
    1393, 1395, 1431, 1436, 1447, 1450, 1464, 1501-1504, 1518-
    1551, 1554-1557
Colorado 7, 956
Connecticut 243, 827

Florida 891-892, 902, 959, 974
Founding Fathers 71, 173, 622-623, 627, 639, 703

Georgia 239, 1313, 1358

Hawaii 1324

Illinois 32, 214, 932, 1160, 1167, 1175, 1181-1182, 1186,
    1191, 1252, 1271, 1318, 1536
Indiana 226, 332, 722, 1032, 1210, 1214, 1238, 1294
Iowa 60, 224, 457, 1050

Jefferson, Thomas 71, 622, 627
Jews 5, 39, 58-59, 84, 148, 177, 233, 1098, 1102, 1251, 1263,
    1342, 1345, 1467

Kansas 130, 371, 960, 962, 999, 1247, 1288
Kentucky 68, 80, 91, 424-425, 529-531, 603, 1547

Madison, James 639
Maine 149, 951
Maryland 250
Massachusetts 78, 220, 388, 832, 1112, 1117, 1142
Michigan 8, 87, 241, 156, 985, 1140, 1242
Minnesota 1287
Missouri 748, 1235, 1249, 1421-1422
Mormons 1462

167